1-800-Oh-My-Goodness

contemporary writs by

CHRIS BENT

www.chrisbent.com

Published in the USA by
Chris Bent
Naples, Florida
USA

http://ChrisBent.com

1-800-I-AM-UNHAPPY,
1-800-FOR-WOMEN-ONLY,
1-800-LAUGHING-OUT-LOUD,
1-800-OH-MY-GOODNESS
1-800-FOR-SEALS-ONLY
and 1-800-BEST-FRIENDS-FOREVER
are trademarks owned by Chris Bent
and are used with his permission.

Also By Chris Bent

Available in Paperback and Electronic Versions

1-800-I-AM-UNHAPPY
Volume 1

1-800-I-AM-UNHAPPY
Volume 2

1-800-FOR-WOMEN-ONLY

1-800-OH-MY-GOODNESS

Coming Soon:

1-800-FOR-SEALS-ONLY

and 1-800-BEST-FRIENDS-FOREVER

DEDICATION

To Christina, Candice, Courtney, and their journeys . . .

Prologue

*This is meant to be a book for just one person. If just that
one person is touched in some way to make their journey
better, then the effort is not in vain. Each one of us can
look back to one moment that changed our direction for the
better. May this book, a collection of my writs and wit, find
that pair of eyes.*

Chris Bent

Kennebunkport
June 2015
www.ChrisBent.com

Contents

Chapters

OMG was just an expression that at first troubled me.

Then I said "why not?" take it on.

Chapter titles came to me during the day and night and I sent them via the "Captio" app and wrote to them at random as inspired. An amazing journey...drawing me more and more into values and what is happening to them.

Then as finishing the notion of doing FSO, 1-800-FOR-SEALS-ONLY came to me. It exploded (pun intended) naturally and was completed in the same month. You will love it.... Unless, of course you don't...

OMG is really directed at you. To be a private companion to making your days more special. There are choices to be made for one to find what they are looking for. This book, hopefully, assists in making those decisions.

I am not preaching. I am just sharing wit and wisdoms that have become more clear to me. After all what else is a 75 year old supposed to do??

Enjoy the journey.

Don't quit on yourself.

1-800-OH-MY-GOODNESS

inspirational writs by

CHRIS BENT

Oh My Goodness

1-800-Oh-My-Goodness was going to be the last book in the 1-800 series but it just keeps coming. LOL

This book will be the most serious and the most challenging. One really has to have read the previous books to have this completely in perspective and to be able to absorb it fully. It challenges you to a critical life decision. It is your life, no one else's.

The title has its own puzzle, especially if you reduce it by one vowel.

I received a few negative comments when using the term OMG in some advertisements. Like, "OMG This place is fabulous!" Or, "OMG, How come I didn't find this place sooner?" I thought a lot about it. Yes, to my generation it is not acceptable. But it is contemporary slang; it is not meant to be disrespectful. And… maybe… just maybe…. It keeps the name God in the vocabulary of the young. A stretch, but a consideration. So bear with me on this journey.

Goodness is the saving grace in life. Right now the world is poised in conflict and evil. Are we just months or a year away from WWIV? Radical Islam against the world? Can we accept and start to deal with evil? Or will it just be a verbal football until it is too late. How many

"It is your life, no one else's."

lives will be lost until we have a course of action?

Goodness is what puts a smile on faces. We need more goodness. We need to act gooder. Our goodness is what we should examine. How good are you? How much good do you do? Are you known for your good? Or your hypocrisy?

Money has nothing to do with good. Achievements are nice. Being a high school quarterback or an award winning intellect or the CEO of a corporation are just achievements. Strip them out of the equation and what is left is how good you are.

You can run the fastest mile and not be the "goodest" guy.

OMG, is that fair…?

So enjoy this journey into the worlds of goodness….

If not… too bad.

Life Seminary

Life sentence.

The most feared penalty of them all...

Everyone wants to live.

Everyone doesn't want to die.

Well, unless you are broke and nobody loves you.

In fact many go through life with only their accomplishments and possessions to define them.... Of course family and friends matter.

But if you want to be recognized you have to get a degree in something... It would be cool if it were Yale or USC or Ohio State or…... We always think people with degrees are better and accordingly more important. Yes we do. Money is important. And his car is important. Important things these; among many.

What happens to your chances of getting a degree, or graduating when you get older and run out of money and friends are dying off? Most of us still have our young minds in the old classroom in our heads. It's another story if there is disease or handicap. The good thing about death is that it doesn't happen until it does...

"Everyone doesn't want to die."

Most of us have done some things that others correctly found abhorrent, or at least very wrong. There is no excuse for sin. It is always our choice.

The biggest sin is self. Self locks one into a personally fulfilling lifestyle. This choice is deadly and wasteful. One never fully appreciates how wrong one was until much later in life. But forgiveness does exist. And one must move beyond and right the wrong. Get beyond self.

There is a spirit of goodness deep within everyone. You have it as a child. Innocence or conscience are the typical labels... But it is much more than that. To most this sounds like nonsense. Too bad. You are wrong.

Entering this world is like entering a classroom. First grade through Final grade. You determine which is the Final grade if you stop going to school.

Quit and you will never know.

I never quit in Hell Week.

And I am still not quitting.

Who would have known there is so much to learn and so much fun ahead for this 75 year old??!!

I have found out that life is a Seminary and I intend to graduate.

The person who will hand me my diploma will be the poorest person I ever served.

Poll Results

The campaigns are over.

The poll results are in.

Nobody likes you.

Okay, the majority doesn't like you.

You are not giving interviews.

How do we get enough opinions from others to know where we stand?

Have we spent enough money with the right people to get us the results we wanted?

We wanted to win.

We wanted everybody to like us.

Damn, we tried so hard.

We got married, we had careers, we retired, we died. A lot more were crying during the eulogy than I had expected. Whew, I guess that is good?? But too late??

We have raised poll taking to a science. Nothing is done any longer

"Nobody likes you."

without a poll to give the enlightened decision makers courage to act. Gut instincts have been totally discredited. Your singular opinion has been totally discredited. Gallup polls, Harris polls, CNN polls, Nielson ratings…. All making big money out of asking stupid questions of thousands to build their databases with assuredness. But… a lot of us answer in shaded manners, interpret differently… polls can be wrong. You can lose your job with the wrong poll information.

Polls can have invisible bias. We have taken morality out of schoolbooks and classrooms. No polls taken in conservative demographics. Morality is prejudicial. No, hard core unbiased statistics guide the money flows. Ha! Wanna bet on it? Only as honest as the CEO…. And we want them to be scandal free and church abiding leaders. Ain't happenin'.

So back to living, guided by the feelings of others as we interpret them… Feelings are driving most everything these days. Poll the feelings and you have a winner.

Tilt. Bad people have feelings. Evil has no feelings. Very complicated.

There has to be a time when there is no time for polls.

Triggers have to be pulled.

The terrorist may just have to be shot.

We can take polls afterwards as to how we feel.

But at least my head was not cut off.

My heart knew what made sense.

I shot him when the polls were closed.

No Sense

What makes sense?

Does falling in love make sense?

In any case, who cares?

It doesn't have to make sense because when it happens nothing else matters at all. Especially logic. So let's start with that irrefutable fact. It is not rocket science. It is not science. It is a fact. Or you belong on some other planet.

Love makes babies. What's not to love? Ok, puppies too. Mothers swear by love. They would die for their child. Go figure? Is this science? No. It just is.

We spend all our life energies seeking love, seeking approval, seeking the things that make us attractive so we can lure love into our life. Cars, houses, vacations, clothes, jewelry….etc. All worms on the love hook… Make sense?

In fact much of what we choose to do makes no sense.

To find out what makes existence tick we now have Facebook and

"Does falling in love make sense?"

Instagram. We seek love through the keyboard. Lemmings finally united. Wanna connect?

Google can explain everything. Science can explain everything. In a way science is like poetry. It traces and explains why things are the way they are back to the beginnings of time. But there is no science as to the beginnings. Our beginnings, our big bang, makes no sense at all. Dead end cliff for the scientist and philosopher. So all we are left with, Ted, is the big argument.

Nothing to worry about anyway. Except…. there remains great disagreement as to how we did begin. I have faith that there is an answer. That answer lies in Faith. So what is wrong with believing in God anyway? All God is about is doing good. Don't you want to do good?

So you scientists who have exhausted science, why not give Faith her just due and try it to see if it answers the unanswerable?

It becomes borderline science if it does.

Is Genesis metaphoric?

Science otherwise is an absolute blast.

The technologies of today are the poetry of the universe.

Where we can go is unimaginable… if we don't kill ourselves along the way.

So let's give our beginnings a little more respect.

Let's have faith in Faith and not put our heads in the sand.

Genesis side or genocide?

Ignorance

"You ignorant fool!

How can you not understand what I am telling you?

How many times do I have to repeat myself to get it into your thick skull??!!"

Hmmm… bet someone once said that to you in some form. Certainly in the military, for sure… and did you ever pay for being stupid.

Ignorance is just not knowing, or it's acting stupid.

If you know then you are really stupid.

Ignorance is used as an excuse by us all. "I just didn't know that would happen." "You can't blame me, I didn't know."

Be it individuals or nations, this excuse does not make things right. How about… "I did not know they would invade." "I did not know so many would be killed." "I had no idea she was abused."

You don't get bailed out with ignorance.

A lot of people avoid religion because of ignorance. They don't know anything about the Bible and don't want anyone else to know how

"You can't blame me, I didn't know."

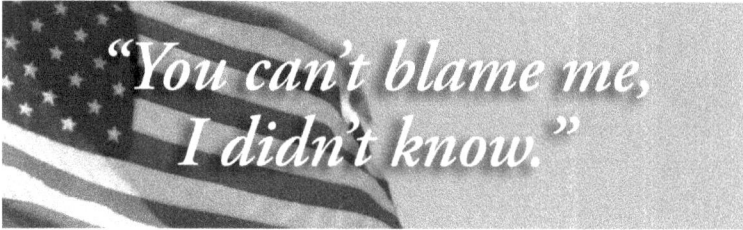

much they don't know. They fear they are supposed to memorize it. Nonsense. It is the spirit of the Word that is important. Religion is meant to set you free, not rule you. Other notions come from ignorance, and plain stupidity. And accepting false notions of what may be expected. Ignorance is deadly to growth. Think about it.

You know how ignorant people are looked down upon? Well, if you choose to be ignorant about Jesus and Christianity then the enemies have won. And you gave them victory. And your life has better odds of mediocrity.

There is nothing wrong with good.

And there is more good in church and Christ than anywhere else.

Don't choose to be an ignorant fool.

You deserve better.

A little learning never hurt anyone.

Hypocrisy

To defend hypocrisy would be hypocritical. Huuhh??

Hypocrisy is a label defining the difference between what one says and what one does.

Few can say they are not guilty.

Most conversation is about what someone else is doing wrong while pretending they're not. Some claim to be better when they secretly are not. We get very angry and disappointed when people we respect let us down. I let people down.

Yet, are we not hypocrites when we judge so finally, and do not allow time for repentance or change? We all change. And if for the better should not they be judged on who they finally became? A lot to think about. To not allow forgiveness is hypocritical. Forgiveness, when earned, is one of life's most powerful and sublime victories.

Now, you and I know we judge others relentlessly. Most parties abound with the hushed whispers of judgment. Just look around, the whisperers are obvious.…

There are hypocrites in church. Church leadership has had their share of pretenders to be beyond reproach while committing crimes of abuse

"To defend hypocrisy would be hypocritical."

and trust. I think many of us allow ourselves the excuse of hypocrisy to disengage from church or our spiritual discovery of goodness. All we see is the hypocrites first and then say we will have no part of anything, any group, any politics, or any church that has one hypocrite in the pew or pulpit.

This is the excuse of the weak or the ignorant as more good is done by those in churches than in any other organizations.

Religion, and specifically Christianity, is the oasis of Truth in life.

Do not use her hypocrites as an excuse not to seek her center, to seek a better person for yourself.

You deserve better.

Find the good, find the strong, find the changed, find the truly knowledgeable.

Never allow hypocrisy to be an obstacle to your destiny.

Never quit.

Find God.

Insecurity

We never tell anyone we are insecure.

We don't want to appear weak.

We are insecure about appearing weak.

We hate it when we are insecure. In fact it drives most everybody. Insecurities about how one looks or comes across, about how much money one has, about capabilities, about strength, about, about, about...... some people are nervous wrecks.... Some people hide it all. The egotistical are the most insecure. You know what I am talking about...

Insecurity makes others feel uncomfortable.

What a monster.

We are drawn to help others with their fears and doubts, with their insecurities. What an honor to be able to make someone feel secure. Husbands to wives, mothers to children. We need insecurity killers. We welcome them. Yet we don't want anyone to know we may be weak...... tough world.

We are also insecure about the whole notion of a God. We don't know what to believe. And we are certainly shy and avoid any discussions for

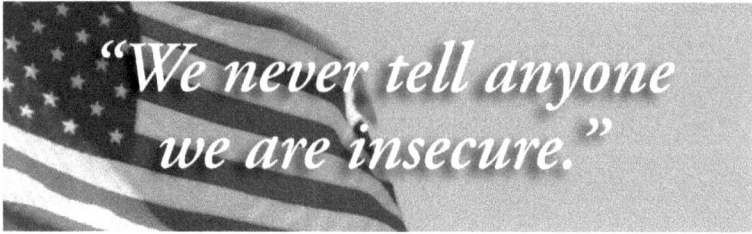

"We never tell anyone we are insecure."

the discomfort they may hold. Insecurity keeps us from being who we could be. It drastically reduces our potential.

So we have to turn to the strong, to those we respect, to those who we know do good, not just talk. Insecurity is a wall between us and a better life. It is a prison of emotions and inaction. Find small good things to do. Compliments, thank yous, errands, hugs, encouragements… small acts have a power of their own.

The more you do the more confident you will become.

This is all about finding God in Goodness.

If you want to live you must not quit.

You must not doubt.

You must never stop working towards Faith.

You are always better than you think.

No insecurity is undefeatable.

Denomination

What is the denomination of that dollar?

I would like it to be a $1,000 bill if there is such a thing?

Would you believe that in 1934 there was issued a Woodrow Wilson $100,000 gold certificate dollar bill!!

You can pay any price for most any denomination.

Let's talk about churches. There are complicated churches with lots of good rules and regulations. There are ones with more music. There are ones with thousands in the pews, and there are those with maybe just 50. Very confusing if not introduced to church by parents. Languages abound. Interpretations abound.

There is a boat to be missed and that is the boat of you. You don't want to sink along the way. You want to make port. Most want to find God if it weren't so difficult and confusing. Of course you could use your heart as a compass, but most no longer trust it. It is the brain and the keyboard that are the unseaworthy vessels these days…

Where to start? Which boat floats? All pastors are not perfect. All priests are not perfect. But when you find one that works for you it is amazing. You light up and know there is truly more to life. When you feel

"All pastors are not perfect."

comfortable, and feel that Spirit of Truth, of Goodness, of Christ… you will know it. Keep searching until you find it.

Do not stay stuck in a church that was not meant for you…. Also don't settle for false gods… Denominations are fabulous, but not if not brought to life for you by the right preaching in the right place.

We are all capable of great goodness, beyond what we comprehend. Humility and unselfishness become the guide when we let go of insecurities, ignorance, and hypocrisy.

This is pretty heavy, but these are heavy times.

I am sorry but the evil in the world needs more people with courage and Faith in the fight.

The time of talking heads is running out of time.

Hey, where is that $100,000 dollar bill??

Rebuild My Smile

No, this is not about plastic surgery.

Some smiles have been made better with plastic surgery, but 99% have not.

Something subtle, but not real.

The illusion of happiness and youth, but something looks funny....

While everybody fawns and says how good you look.

I am sorry, but heart surgery is needed to correct a smile. Years of anguish, disappointment, pain, and tragedy steals the soul from the lips. Faces defaced. Big money spent. False hopes dashed. Trust damaged. Mirrors avoided. The only thing left is heart surgery.

Of a different sort.

When there is joy deep within, it cannot be contained. Every pore of one's being exudes something special. Something happy. There is a sparkle back in the eyes. Even the damaged face no longer cares. Laughter is in the air. The smile is genuine. Really genuine, not a surface face smile.

So great surgeon, how do I find you? Where is your office? What are

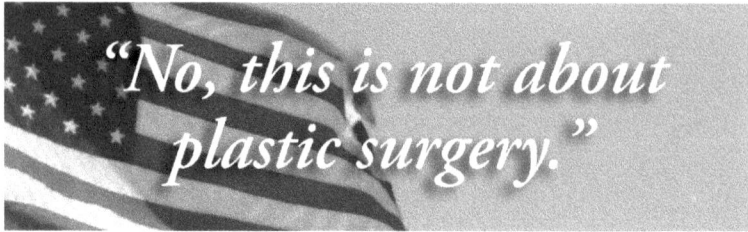

your hours? I can wait. I can stand in line. A friend can take me there.

The place is called the Clinic Of Others. You just go there and there will be hundreds of people you can help. If you agree and sign the form you will be assigned your first 20. You won't have time for yourself. You will have no time for the mirror. You will come home tired and happy at having given so much of yourself to strangers!!

The Spirit of Christ is what empowers you to persevere and see each person to the end. Until you must part and move on to the next. Just helping with encouragement, insight, and compassion.

This fuel is found nowhere else. Of course your intellect says otherwise, but your heart is where the solution lies.

Your smile will be rebuilt.

You will never have to look at yourself again, nor care what others see.

You will be who you were meant to be.

Maybe even an angel.....

Prisoner Exchange

Sometimes one is taken hostage by evil.

Sometimes it may be a family member or a friend.

Sometimes it gets personal.

Otherwise it is just something bad that happens to someone else on the news.

Sometimes a bad person can be exchanged for a good person.

But these days evil seems to trump reason.

What if you are a prisoner of an addiction or of bad behavior or of just being selfish? What if you are a prisoner of pride? Or of money? Or of poverty?

Who can you get to make the exchange for you? For us?

Our values are becoming a prisoner of keyboards. Keystrokes are abducting our youth and taking them to a cyber-prison of illusion. How do we hack in and rescue them?

Talking heads on TV are debating and stealing our intellects with doubts, confusion, and half-truths.

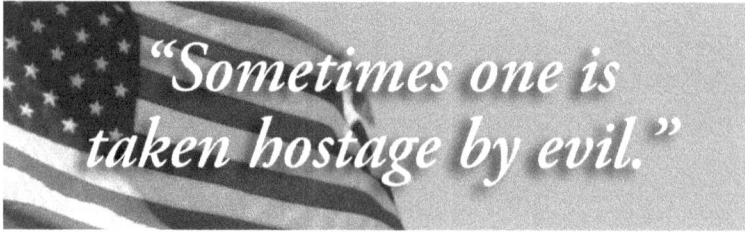

"Sometimes one is taken hostage by evil."

The political parties look like they will take no prisoners as the campaigns start.

Some special leader needs to emerge and identify Himself.

Who is it going to be?

Is He one of us??

Classic Radio

I have a friend who started working on an AM radio station in Biddeford, Maine in the late 50's.

I just met him a couple of years ago.

Now with Sirius/XM satellite radio one can get most anything via Wi-Fi.

I have discovered Radio Classics. In the 40's and 50's radio was in its prime. There was comedy, mysteries, westerns, science fiction…. Unimaginable experiences for a young boy. Flights of fantasy. Suspense, Johnny Dollar, X Minus One, Bob Hope, Jack Benny, The Shadow, Green Hornet, Gunsmoke, The Lone Ranger, the Whistler, Lights Out, Sherlock Holmes……….endless fun.

Now, when at the pool armed with my ear buds and iPhone I am reliving my childhood.

I know you will say "how dumb, how old, how retirement home, how boring"…

The astounding thing is, the jokes and timing and spins on meaning are fabulous. The total lack of sexual language revealed humor at its zenith. It is so refreshing to listen to clean humor. Bizarre that it has any value

as humor at all. But these guys and their writers were better than we are today….. Amazing and funny.

As to all the other genres it was always about good and evil, selfishness, pride, greed and murder. But the beauty was that things were black and white. You kinda learned what was good and what was bad as the heroes reflected to themselves. You could almost get a PHD in values from all these tales. Inventive sound effects, walking steps, creaking doors, gunshots, screams, and canned laughter! It all worked! It seems so stupid. But it really was entertaining as you closed your eyes and were transported into other worlds as you imagined them… Amazing virtual realities inside your brain.

Yes, classic radio fathered a generation of children. Challenged their imaginations, and ultimately sent them into real life to all the corners of the world.

Along came television and imaginations became controlled. Oh, in the early days of television it was pretty clean and exciting. Black and white on screen and stories about good and bad, all black and white. Then came color and its glorious rainbows of reality. Look where we are today! HD TV, 3D TV with picture quality never imagined.

Except that it has taken our sense of right and wrong into mega-confusion. Values are lost in feelings.

Actors become role models of lifestyle.

Where have all the heroes gone?

Athlete's flaws are revealed, obscuring their greatness.

OMG where has Classic radio gone?

Long time passing………

Peter, Paul, and Mary??

Perfecting Imperfection

Mirrors.

Reflections of truth or….. imperfection?

The only way you can look at yourself eye to eye.

Why do you wish to see more than you do?

Why does the eye go to the imperfection first?

If it goes to the perfect then you are really vain.

And have no clue what is due…..

Boy, do blondes look great! But if you look at their roots one might see that it is not permanent… hmmm… What to wear so I look better? Which color is best on me? Are the pants too short? I can change how this looks by…..?

By trying to compensate for the perceived imperfection… The money spent on trying to change our psychological and physical flaws is the largest expenditure of mankind, except for food and war.

There is one place in man that is perfect. The heart. The center of all feeling and Truth. Yes, physical hearts get disease and are less than perfect. They need stents, a bypass, pacemakers… and even

"Why does the eye go to the imperfection first?"

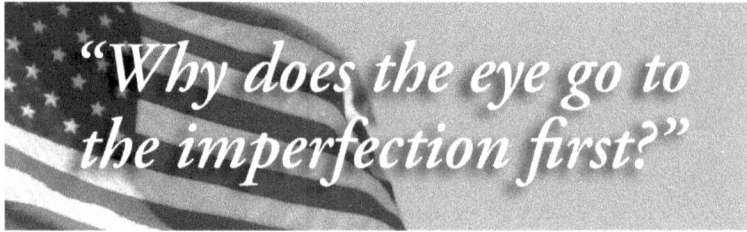

transplants.... But that is not the heart we are addressing. The most central part of our being is not the brain, but the heart. Truth dictates guilt. Truth dictates insecurity. Moral Truth.

We waste so much time and energy fretting over imperfection. Plastic surgery is an extreme form of the inability to embrace life in Truth. And it seldom looks perfect. Big gamble, these superficial remedies. So is the yacht, the car, the spoils of wealth. So are drugs and alcohol and sloth and greed and pride and lust.

Imperfection disappears when you are no longer the center of you.

You can only be found in the act of helping others.

This requires spiritual surgery.

The operation is called Faith.

Want to feel totally excited?

Create a genuine smile on the face of someone in need.

You will never need a mirror again.

You will have perfected imperfection.

Read My Lips

Now if that isn't a famous quote.

If it was by Clint it was great.

It was great when said by George.

"Make my day and draw." If you can't hear what they are saying you better be able to read lips. We all know a few expressions by lips. Some are just two words. Love or hate, we can read the lips. But what about the ones we miss???

Lips can say the darndest, deadliest and loveliest things imaginable. It is just up to our imaginations or feelings to utter them. Ever tried to see what someone else was whispering across the room?? We waste half our lives in this futile pursuit. And most of the time we get it wrong. Just one word missed and we get the worst interpretation.

The devil says "Make my day!". Get it?

Flash of brilliance. The movement of lips are inconsequential if you know and Trust the person. You can look away and know what they are saying. Like you have eyes in the back of your head. Trust, respect, and love come from a closeness that life and heart has brought you.

"Make my day and draw."

Soldiers in combat entrust their existences to one another. Night vision goggles don't show lips. Silence is golden. Very.

Sometimes there is just not time for conversation or words. Action is required instantly. Dogs get it. We humans want time to analyze everything. Disrespect, evil, and danger all require immediate response. Any delay risks life and learning.

Parents, schools, and governments often risk undermining the foundation of a healthy society by inaction and delayed discipline. We have taken Trust out of the equation.

I don't think we can read the lips when someone says "I don't trust you.".

We can all read lips when someone says "I love you.".

Why, because that is what we most want to hear.

Make your day.

Read the Red Print.

Forever Now

Now.

I want it now.

Now or never.

The only thing we know of life is now. The past moment is over. The next moment is yet unseen. Oops, here it is. Each new word on this page is a new moment, a new now. Crazy.

We love to anticipate the next pleasing event and we love to worry about the less pleasing… Can't wait till it arrives?

Except the only moment that matters is right now. This keystroke. This gift.

This conversation. Will it lead somewhere? Where is the motivation coming from? We only live in the now. Our past "nows" determine our success, our happiness. We must make the most of every now. That defines existence.

In the moments of happy we want them to last forever. The great feeling of happy drives us to create the next one. If we had our way happy "nows" would be forever.

"Do you want forever happy?"

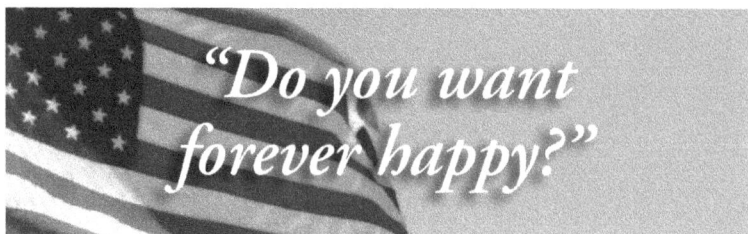

What about the "nows" that are full of pain, of remorse, of physical disease or even worse, torture or even worse, abuse? We desperately want those "nows" to cease immediately. Except we don't know how. And often we keep repeating ourselves, repeating the causes, and repeating the pain…with no way out seen. Forever never?

"Hope springs eternal." What does that mean? It means it is human nature to never give up hope. Hope is powerful. Hope is a form of faith. A faith that there is better, that there is redemption. Then it becomes Faith.

If one can find Faith… which requires a total commitment, not just a brain journey… then one has a path to finding happier moments and a return to the zone of happy.

Once you taste happy again you can choose to not make the same mistakes.

Your choice alone.

Do you want forever happy?

Commit and find out.

Help someone who has lost hope.

Love At First Sight

Cupid is an angel?

What does the head of a baby look like as it emerges from the womb into its first light and breath?

The tears of pain from the mother's cheeks fall on this head.

It is love at first sight.

She is the first to love her child.

The bond to the mother is hereby cemented into eternity.

"Where is my mommy?" is a primordial cry since time began. And still remains hidden today in the pain of the living, of the lost, the lonely... This cry remains hidden deep within for life. Grownups don't want to admit it....

A mother could have been lacking or lost in the abandonments of life. Even then..... some day she will be understood, loved more, and even forgiven, and loved even more.

We do not choose our mothers. Cupid does.

If life is tough or we go down the selfish road, love becomes the only

"We do not choose our mothers."

thing we trust or are drawn to. The emotions of love are so magically compelling and transcend all logic. In the attraction phase we totally yield to feelings, both heartfelt and physical. Holding hands as if there were not a care in the world. If blessed, ...holding hands at death.

We can give birth to all kinds of goodness. We can hold hands and guide others. Their love will be felt in our private pride. Knowing you helped is knowing you loved. You don't have to sleep with or marry every person you love.

Looking across a room you can feel drawn to a beautiful woman or a strong man. It is so exciting to feel love at first sight..... even if it is only for a night?

No, the love we are talking about is deeper, more substantive.

You will give up your life for your child.

I would.

Would you send your Son to die?

Someone did.

Blue Prayer

A dot on the blue.

A boat.

A blue line from horizon to horizon.

A white cloud.

Above and below.

Slip into the silence.

Face mask narrowing vision to what is in front of you. Pulling, compelling, awe invoking.

Beauty humbles. Close to heaven.

The world underneath the surface of the blue water becomes a prayer. Corals shaped by the random whimsy of unseen nature.

Colors of new rainbows.

Fish swimming in and out with the freedom humans know not. Iridescent lines of verse. Glorifying Creation.

One gently glides one's fins to explore the next 6 feet, senses heightened to the unexpected. Which is always.

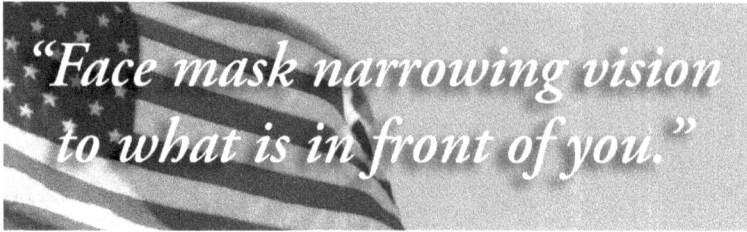

Deeper is darker. Foreboding… yet calling one to dare….

Shallower is brighter… where color explodes. Intensities unseen above. Only in the churches of the oceans.

The only sounds being the parrot fish crunching the coral…. And of course, your bubbles. Your bubbles disturbing the holy serenity.

With skill and new gear no bubbles are near. And silence is again married to silence.

Man floats weightless like in space in liquid. Weightless is a cathedral of its own. Except… kneeling is without effort.

Man has just begun to see and map all the beauty. Is not beauty sometimes best left alone? Like the innocence of a child. Who wants to be the first to steal it? No one.

But we do. We swim through life unaware of the stems broken off the coral. Of the people we ignore with an unseen rudeness. With small hurts rendered indifferently.

We take care of ourselves first.

Priority me. Not Thee.

Find that small boat in the vastness of the blue.

Bobbing in the blue horizon.

Unseen but by the fish below.

And say a prayer.

A blue one.

OMG.

Angelfish

What does an angel look like?

Have you known one?

Or are they just winged figures on the ceilings of the Vatican?

So many angels are never seen….

Maybe because we don't want to or just don't believe in what is not on Facebook…

If you slide into the blue water beneath your boat over a coral reef somewhere you come across an amazingly flat graceful angel. Not edible, just beautiful. What a blessing to see one, to see that their uniqueness was created somehow. Somehow?

Tiny ones can be found in aquariums, delighting the eyes of children. Very large ones in oceans everywhere. "Mommy, are angels fish?"

Like in life you have to fish for angels. You have to know where to look. Under the surface. Wherein sings a soul existing for others.

Angels are everywhere

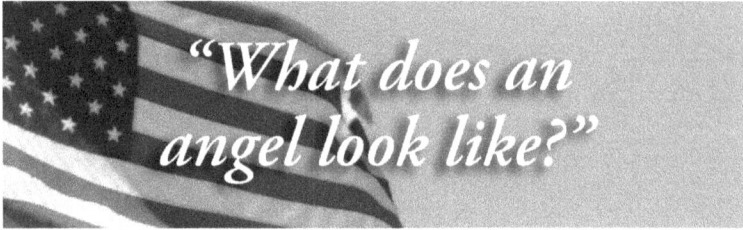

"What does an angel look like?"

Open your eyes and believe.

And say a prayer.

A blue one.

OMG.

GPS

Orienteering is the skill of navigating over land and forest with a compass and a terrain map…

Waypoints are marked on trees and all you have is a compass and map to help you try to find it.

Really fun if getting somewhere matters.

We used our underwater compass to direct us towards ships at night. Dark harbors, oxygen rebreathers, no bubbles. Have to come up several times to make sure your course was good. Then you had to commit and swim until you felt the hull. Spooky if you didn't love it.

Finding your way. Today? Well it is GPS all the way. Everyone knows exactly where they are all the way. Destinations can be marked and viewed via satellite.

The kids say today in amazement "You used a compass? What is that??" Duuhh, I don't know…

Some destinations are really important to find. Targets especially when evil exists. Even Amazon is talking about delivering pizza via GPS drones. Go figure?

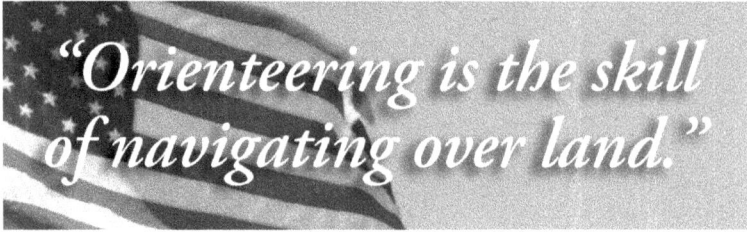
"Orienteering is the skill of navigating over land."

We have all the answers. And they are all digital.

Moral certitude. Now that is a complicated destination. Most don't care to know that it could even be on one's map. But if nobody gets there, then society will cease to exist. Huuuhh?

There are courses to take and ones to avoid. Our problem is we want "easy" and we want "feel-good". We want to make sure we are happy and are not cheated out of pleasures that others get to enjoy. So our compass just spins as it is caught by false magnets. Dizzy confusion. Where is true north? Where is True?

True can be found on the road to Faith. It is uphill. The road is filled with sweat and doubt. No compass is needed. No GPS is needed. Our heart tells us what is right and wrong.

Why don't we follow it?

Who makes this compass?

In heaven?

Valentine

Red heart.

For my valentine.

My heart is red, I think.

It makes my red liquid go where it is needed.

From foot to head.

My heart is everything.

I even get to give it away kinda when love invades reason.

Everybody wants someone else's heart. We try to be noticeable to other's eyes. We smile and laugh. Heart magic we play.

You have to have heart to be someone. Without heart you are no one. You don't matter. Nobody will care about you. You will be very alone with self. You will be insecure and angry. You will pretend otherwise. Others can tell easily. Heartless.

"You gotta have heart!" goes the song.

How do you get heart?

Hold a child. Does the innocence compel you to protect it at all costs? Even with your life? Not courage but a deep compulsion to act regardless the cost. It has to be your heart telling you what is right and wrong. You have to let it.

Your heart sees what your eyes can't.

You can be a valentine to someone else every day if you make them smile. Every day can be February 14 with a little imagination. Not cards, but words that hug. Or a hug at the right moment. Your heart will tell you when.

If you can create a laugh for others then you are Wholly red.

It's ok to die for someone else.

Die to self.

Let me valentine you.

Happy Valentine's Day.

Eye Pain

"You are a pain in the eye".

An eyesore.

Something that is not fun to look at….. Don't take it personally….but there are those who think so….

Turn on the old TV, well I mean the new 55" Curved OLED ½ inch flat screen with stunning crispness and color…

You can see everything but that which is important. And the sound? You can get truly lost in this TV… Which is what happens when you watch most movies, news, and whatever. Truly lost.

It is comforting to be able to be detached with a couple of beers and chips and mightily taking on the evening news. Regardless of whether it is telling the truth…. All the diverse opinions insure we are confused and entertained.

To me this is eye pain… hey, let's make it one word, "eyepain"…. Or maybe EP…?

Wait, if we can't look at the pain how will we know if it is getting closer? What about all the pain that is being caused by abuse…. or torture… or abandoned families?

"You are a pain in the eye."

It's one thing to look at pain. Is it not another to feel it? To be the victim? To know the horror of the aloneness of pain? Separated from all love?

There is pain all around us. Pain that is not on a screen. Pain that is hidden deep within. Sometimes you can see it in a side glance of a face, the twitch of an eye, the furrow of a brow. Usually the eyes will hint at eye pain.

But there is a more important eye. It is called the heart. Funny how you can just feel things sometimes. Not intuition but a real sense of something… pain, danger, evil.

When a man grows up and starts to forget about himself. When he finds that helping others relieves him of himself. When he finds that there is more to the heart than meets the eye. Then, and only then will he feel all the pain around him every day. Pain that others are secretly hiding.

He will reach out in whatever way available.

An unexpected hug or a "God Bless You"…

In some small way he will take on the battle of pain.

He will die to himself on other's crosses.

Noble and humble.

He will have become a man.

One Laugh

One laugh.

In Las Vegas you can pay a fortune to get one laugh.

That's all you ask for.

More would be fantastic.

A great comedian has promised an evening of laughter.

But you will settle for even just one laugh.

The old days had Bob Hope and Jack Benny for starters. Their twist of meaning was like the finest of laugh wines. Clean and unexpected. Jimmy Fallon is pretty good these days. All it takes is one laugh to make you feel better.

It's great to have a laugh at work. Relieves the pressure. It's great when a boss makes you laugh… if it is funny… Why does laughter make everyone feel comfortable? Why? OK, it just does… don't have to analyze…

When you first meet someone and they make you laugh you think they are good. Of course, some people are just good at it. And some good people are not. I don't care… make me laugh. I'll stay up to 11:30 to get one from the Tonight Show.

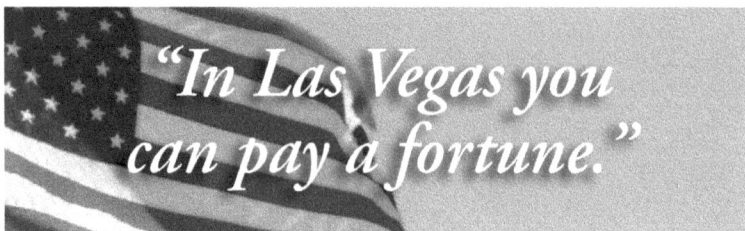

There are people all around us, within feet who have worries you can't imagine. They don't tell anyone. We get real good at hiding it. It's called the Worry Cover-up. It eats at you. Being busy helps. Having the kids screaming even helps. Distractions help. Anything helps.

All it would take is just one laugh at the right time. Instant relief. Rolaids for the soul. Nice if they could come in packs of ten.

Humor can be found in every moment if you care for others. It just comes in a micro-second when you feel their need. Silliness, innocent silliness. Just a flash of it can transform a moment into a celebration of a sparkling eye or the wiping of an inner tear.

One laugh, that's all it takes.

Let go.

Be a one laugh person.

And transform the world.

Who said love wasn't funny?

American Sniper

American Sniper is a movie made from a book by a real person.

It is biographical non-fiction.

The author was murdered.

Chris Kyle was a good man.

A very good man.

His murderer was sick and evil and one of us.

This movie is proving to be one of the all-time largest grossing films. All its competition are fantasy fiction movies. All are pure entertainment and escapes from reality.

American Sniper is not. Its greatness and appeal is from confronting issues head on with artistic realism. We are forced into conversations that all other movies avoid. What to do about evil? Who can do something about it? Does evil exist? We get criticized if we try to define what is good or bad. Sad state of affairs.

The movie makes us think about what military families give up for us. The movie provides moral dilemmas facing the soldier. It is not impersonal but personal. Memories haunted by acts of horror and doubt.

"A choice that terrifies..."

We have Navy SEALs to do some special assignments in the quiet. Risk taking at the extreme. Beyond conventional boundaries. Special Warfare is special. Training is beyond imagination. You know nothing about it.

The movie misses giving us a real feeling of the exhaustion and pain endured. Hell week is a week of indescribable fortitude and compromise. You have to give up your being to trust. Trust that you will not die. You may quit at any time. A choice that terrifies you every moment.

Leaders are forged.

They know what it takes.

Moral leadership requires moral leadership.

The world needs us.

"Quitting is not an option."

Forever Silent

What do we know about what we don't know about?

How can we judge when we don't know the whole Truth?

But judge we do, and fervently claim we are right.

Do we have heroes we never know about?

The submariner's Silent Service?

The CIA operative?

The Green Beret alone out there?

The Stealth flight that never existed?

The SEAL returning unseen?

The private pain of a veteran?

The tear of a wife?

Heroes in humility.

Keeping us free.

Allowing us to smile.

"Who pins the medals on them?"

Who pins the medals on them?

We will never know.

They want it that way.

God Bless America.

No AC

No AC.

You mean no air conditioning??

OMG, what are we going to do?

I am not going to work.

I'll go sit in the car until you get it fixed!

Yes, summers in St. Louis, Philadelphia, and New York City get mighty hot. Sweltering. Steam on the pavements hot. All one can think of is the beach or autumn. In fact you beg for deep snow... kinda...

One can travel to Egypt. One can travel to the Vatican. One can travel to Moscow, London, Paris, Mexico City, or Jerusalem... and find amazing structures, amazing buildings, and more than amazing churches.

Oops, they had no computers, no typewriters, no phones, no trucks. Yet they built and built in unimaginable testimony to the potential of man. Today they are being bombed to rubble in wars far away. Evil hates accomplishment.

How did they do it? The Duomo in Milan with her handset arches

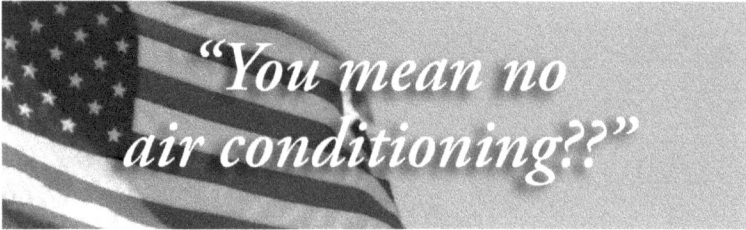

with her unique precision stones is just art. Hey, no power tools or forklifts…. Amazing…. Today we have so many committees and building codes that no grandeur would have been possible.

Man worked like an ant to raise his imagination toward the heavens. Pyramids.

But most disturbing and logic defying of them all was it was done with No AC! No Poland Spring bottled water. No sanitizer. No paper towels. No aspirin.

But no air conditioning???!!! They had to be crazy. Insane crazy.

But maybe, … they just had no choice. Maybe they had no clue of what was better. Maybe not knowing is better than knowing….

They did great in spite of no AC, go figure.

Today is a very dangerous time. Evil abounds, unless your head is in some ideological sand. We don't want to sweat. We want machines and computers to do things for us. Oh, just send in the SEALs. They will do our sweaty work for us. Let others bleed as long as it is just on TV.

Imagine the world we could build if we had a dream?

If the artist in us was freed to worship and be?

Turn off the TV.

Put the phone down.

And go outside where there is no AC.

Demand from our leaders that we be set free.

Again.

Blackface

Al Jolson did not look natural with black makeup back in the black and white film era.

He was called The World's Greatest Entertainer.

His singing had its own style.

It was good entertainment, but what right does a white man have to portray a black person?

Black makeup covering the obvious Caucasian. The black man had suffered enough. Yet, the white man had suffered enough when he left Europe… Who has not suffered?

Suffering is evil. It is not good. It can make you stronger. But we all envision a world without suffering where fairness and justice rule. Compassion and Truth reside in a good society. And Truth is determined by goodness and kindness and love, not by edict and discrimination. Faces must be free of concealment and arrogance.

Our faces are meant to entertain, to show love and happiness and sorrow and hope. How can every face be so unique? Like the stars in the heavens. None should ever be hidden. Only evil hides … until it commits its desecrations…

The face of evil hides behind many makeups. It can hide in religion and in government. People make evil happen. Some can be smiling while planning death. Evil is not a debate in a classroom. It beheads good when we look away.

Evil makes women slaves of involuntary sex. Evil dehumanizes mankind. Evil destroys a child in the womb. Evil makes a child fatherless.

Evil is a real, not imagined enemy.

It only yields in the face of great force.

Atomic?

If we don't declare war will we skirmish ourselves to death?

We can only be great if united.

Black and white we must fight.

Singing "Mammy".

Never Die

Who wants to die?

"Not I" quoth the raven.

If I go to battle I choose not to die.

I want to grow very old and stay very healthy.

There is so much advice on how to be smiling, and healthy, way into your 90's. Love promises are in abundance.

I can't wait to get older as it looks like so much fun. Doctors are specialists in everything that could be a nuisance. Community living until the First Class bus to heaven. No sweat.

OK, I really never want to die. What about you? Is dying the same as not being remembered? If you are not remembered what is the point to life? And remembered for what? Getting real complicated. Most want everything easy and not complicated…

Bad people are remembered. Do you want to be remembered as bad? Does that make you evil? Yep, goes with the terrain. And your bad will be associated with all your offspring forever… on the internet. Google your bad and everyone can find it and a picture of your bad face. Hell?

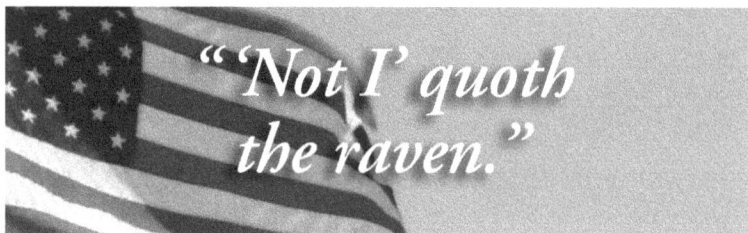

" 'Not I' quoth the raven."

You won't be remembered for being mediocre. And for not finishing on a high note. There has to be more to retirement than retirement?

There is if you find a way… Work at a way to mean something to someone else.

Funny how we don't forget when someone is nice to us.

Even the smallest things have meaning.

The problem is that "self" gets in the way. "Self" screws it all up.

Because the other person feels your ego and your insecurity as you do something for yourself.

You are nobody until others are more important to you than yourself. You can't find your true self on the golf course or at the baseball game… unless of course, you are taking someone in need….. however loosely defined.

You can be remembered forever as the person who cared. Really cared.

No, writing a check doesn't count.

You can live in the heart of another, or a family, if your humility allows you think outside of yourself.

To know that others really are more important.

That they are the food for the soul.

The fountain of youth lies therein.

"Nevermore" quoth the Raven.

Never Forget

Never forget the atrocities of World War II, of December 7, of September 11.

The beheadings of 2015.

There are dates that will never be forgotten when evil took the life of a daughter or son.

No one wants to have such dates in one's past. Never.

We never forget our first love. We never forget our first dog. We never forget our high school classmates, unless the class is too big… We never forget our first car, our first job, or a parent's death.

Forgetting can be a tool of the lazy. Forgetting can be a byproduct of information overload. Forgetting can be intentional.

One thing we seldom forget is when we have lied to someone else. I remember.

One thing we never forget is when we have hurt someone else. We pretend it never happened by avoiding thinking about it… but deep down the human being does not forget. Oh, some can, but it is a dangerous game they are playing with their self. Guilt never abates until

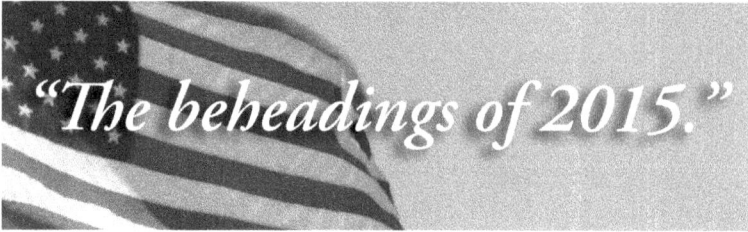

"The beheadings of 2015."

forgiven. Alcoholism and substance abuse and violence are false escapes from Truth.

Loneliness is not forgotten as it reaches deep. Appearances attempt to hide these pains, but they are just masks held on by thin elastic.

You also never forget when someone is kind to you.

When you are caring for someone else you do not forget it. You do not forget the warm humble feeling of having helped. You are not forgotten.

The "not-forgotten" world can be one of good and accomplishment and serenity. When bad is done it carries pain that is hard to forget. However, when good is done it feels good. It is right. It is powerful. It can trump bad.

A child remembers seeing good deeds as it forms its sense of fairness.

A vision of right must be nourished… not visions of fear.

Only we can create the world that should not be forgotten.

It is our choice to choose what to never forget.

It might take fighting for.

Constitution

My constitution is fine.

I am feeling better.

I am a lot older and had heart surgeries, but have really changed my diet and exercising again

I feel surprisingly good. My constitution is back to normal.

Less alcohol, less white bread, less sugar, less eating…..

It works.

What we do with ourselves determines our constitution. How we feel about our self. If we remain centered in self, we just will not feel good even though we pretend otherwise. The best and only food for a good constitution is helping others. Each time you try it you will like it.

There are really rules if you want to feel good, if you want to have a good constitution. There has to be some church with some pastor who can resonate with you. Try, and try to find him or her. Don't quit. Don't prejudge; it is its own arrogance.

We need healthy and wise citizens to lead us out of our bickering political chaos. We need to stop amending our Constitution so it is

"I feel surprisingly good."

more politically correct. The spirit of our Constitution has served us more than well. There is nothing wrong with it. Fine print cures nothing.

Our founding fathers used Christian principle as our cornerstones. History affirms its solidity. We have fought so many wars trying to protect the inalienable rights we hold dear. We are going to have to fight again soon. Islam rejects our values and culture. We have to stop debating otherwise. We can live in peace only when Islam chooses to champion peaceful co-existence.

Their leaders have to show some leadership or the price paid will be high.

Where is their Constitution that affirms inalienable rights?

Respect and freedom for women.

What century do they live in?

We need peace and honesty for all.

Evil must be recognized for what it is.

EVIL.

Post Office

When you are young things are just more fun.

Games are more fun.

Playing is more fun.

Even adults are more fun because they are nice to you.

There was a game called Post Office. It was a kissing game where the boys were in one room and the girls in another. A boy would bring a letter into the room with the girls and receive a kiss stamp from each. Each boy would repeat, then each girl would do same. Lots of kisses and lots of fun. Delivering the mail was never better.

Then there was a Post Office game where you made a line of friends and whispered something in the first person's ear who then repeated it to the person next to him... And after 10 people had passed it on the last would repeat what he had heard out loud. It usually bore little resemblance to the original message.

Not a very good post office are we….. maybe every time you tell someone something, things happen to the truth……. Like maybe even the evening news has gone through filters???

"Games are more fun."

Maybe even history books have gone through many interpretations. How do we know what really was the cause of a war?

The USPS, aka, the United States Postal Service, formerly known as just the "Post Office" has become a monster. Not to say that our mail always gets there, but it is something that you can count on… and that is fantastic.

But it loses scandalous amounts of money. It has refined bureaucracy into an art. Jobs for life. Be very careful and plodding, not breaking any rule and you can make it to the end and a wonderful pension… plus innumerable days off….. Entitlement perfected. UPS doesn't lose money? Go figure.

So much good could be achieved if government bureaucracies weren't so fat and allowed to languish behind their walls of fine print and approval hierarchies.

Why can't we do better?

Why is private industry scorned for making money efficiently and government praised for losing money? Renewable energy renews itself on subsidy and theft from the citizen.

We talk around the truth and continue to bury the future before it is born.

We will need money to fight the next war. Where are we getting it???

Politics is making the theft camouflaged by earmarks and partisan praise.

We are becoming incoherent.

Whisper it to the person next to you.

You've Got Mail

I love getting mail.

Especially in the old days when they had stamps on them.

So exciting to open and read the handwritten note.

 Especially if the sender might love you.

Soldiers used to stand in line at mail call.

They could be in any dark place in the world. They would rush to some private dirt corner and read as if they were in heaven. Isn't that where love letters come from anyway?

Times have changed. Fountain pens don't sell like they used to. Everything is typed. Even Valentine cards have the love letter pre-written so all you have to do is sign.

I now love getting to my office and opening up AOL. "You've got mail" is said by a pleasant male voice. It is exciting to know that some people are sending you mail even though they don't love you. It sounds so wonderful… "You've got mail!"

When I open my mail on my iPhone or iPad there is no voice…

"I love getting mail."

My daughter gave me this wonderful picture of her son. It has a motion sensor, and this very young voice, my Grandson's, says "I love you.".

We all need mail that is not bills or offers disguised as something else. Sadly, mail is now electronic... or is it? Texting allows one to stay in closer communication with others than ever before. It is sure wonderful with friends. Not exactly letters, but alive and in the "now".

Twitter, facebook, Skype, etc. are almost lettering us to death.

Heads are always down.

Will we ever learn to look up again??

"You've got Mail".

That's Life

If you can sing...

You might know of an old guy named Frank Sinatra.

If you do, then "That's Life" had touched your soul.

It's worth playing over and over until you get the message that life is what it is and you can always try again. Pick yourself up and go for it. Keep going for it.

We give up too often, always judging the future.... Much less the next moment. It is human nature.

It is human nature to want to fall in love. It is human nature to get into trouble. It is human nature for the young to think they are smarter than they are. It is human nature for the old to think they are smarter than they are.

Humility is the only thing that makes one smart. For with humility you listen and you learn. Humble people see more around them than non-humble people do. In fact, non-humble people are mostly blind to what is going on around them. Same goes for politicians. Same goes for nations.

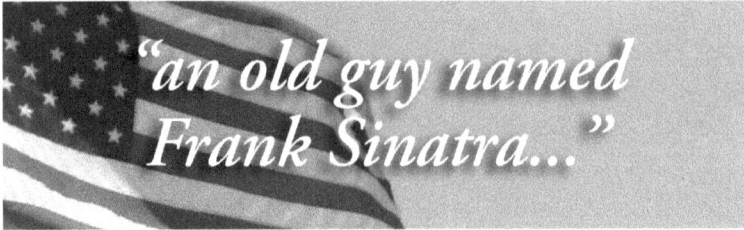

"an old guy named Frank Sinatra..."

If humility were a stock on Wall Street I would put all my money in it. I want to be bonded to it. LOL.

How do you buy it?

The answer is with pain. Growing up poor. Or experiencing poverty. If arrogant, one has to be brought way down to gain it. It is something that sadly requires prayer you guys…. Sorry but That's Life.

One has to be able to see and feel other's pain to claim humility.

Then you will know what you have to do in life.

Your path will finally be clear.

And you will find peace in serving others.

For without service you languish in irrelevance.

That's Life.

If Only

If….

If only…..

If only I had not said that.

If only I did not give up.

She would still be with me.

Yes, my dream.

My childhood dream to be someone. My childhood dream to have or do something.

No regrets? Hard to think of a person who does not have one. Some say they had no choice. Maybe it was true. But most know the truth deep inside… there was a choice along the way.

If only I had known better. If I had not turned my head the other way. If I had not tuned out the advice offered by so many. I did not want to listen to advice from a live person trying to help me with my journey.

I texted and Google searched for the answer, for advice from my keyboard. Something was missing from the keyboard. Some invisible poignancy. Some sense of caring not digitalized.

"If only I had not said that."

Text me up Scotty!

I no longer want to look at myself in a face-book.

I need to look at me in a mirror.

I need to take my sunglasses off.

I need to see my eyes.

I need to see my heart.

If only someone had told me this sooner.

Evil Pastor

There once was a pastor named Evil.

He didn't ride motorcycles.

But he jumped the canyons of the mind.

Taking us to the abyss as if we were blind.

How often do we do things not fully realizing the implications?

Being impulse-driven for a moment often creates the hangover in the morning, and a subtle deep guilt.

"Let's hang out somewhere." Hangover assured.

Nobody intends to hurt another, but irresponsible behavior usually is a part of the party. Someone gets hurt.

One's vision of a safe and promising place to explore is often naïve and dangerous. Travel to some exotic regions are fraught with perilous odds. Leave this country and much unseen evil brushes by you. You may be making merry right next to a person not akin to your beliefs. You have no clue what danger lurks next to you.

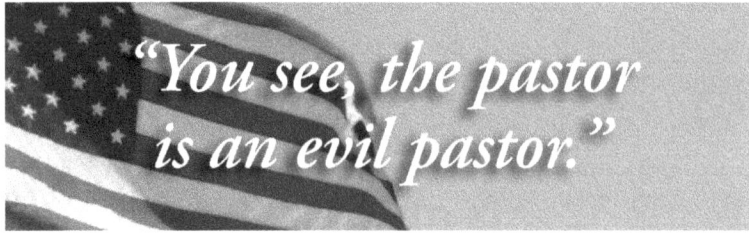
"*You see, the pastor is an evil pastor.*"

Warnings in the media not heeded. "Can't happen to me" until your life is pleaded for by your parents.

We look at churches and their pastors as symbolic of some old, uninformed culture. A hangout for the duped.

What we don't give consideration to is that their profession is really about evil. Their sole focus is on preventing evil, stopping it in its tracks. They are the professionals as sin starts inside the self. Indifference to others creates the soil of lies, greed, and hideous acts. At the heart of evil is terror. Pulpits ring every Sunday with unheeded warnings. NIMBY, Not In My Back Yard, is the protection most all hide behind. It is happening elsewhere, but not near me.... So no one prepares for evil.

Terror in a shopping mall or school is very evil. But if you want to get to its source you have to listen to the preacher. The Bible has so many examples of goodness and right. And how to be a strong person in the face of temptation and evil.

You see, the pastor is an evil pastor, and evil preacher, as he tells us how evil evil is. He is the expert on evil. He has seen it in the tears of the countless and the hearts of the broken.

Let a pastor teach you of evil.

Protect someone.

Learn to see evil before it starts.

Say No when it matters.

Immediately.

Air Guitar

Imagine a song being called "Imagine".

Written by a John Lennon?

You have had two glasses of wine.

Feel just right.

Nice.

She is in the room with you.

You pick her up.

And strum and pick the chords as if you were John.

Smile on your face.

Your eyes are closed.

Imagination taking you anywhere music is played.

It feels good imagining.

Imagining a world where wherever you go 2 glasses makes all glow.

You see fire and you see pain.

You see drought and you see rain.

Your instrument is always there.

Wonder what is up above so very far?

Is it a harp or your air guitar?

Come Across

She yells "It's okay, come across!"

The water is shallow and the coral is sharp.

The suspension bridge is just rope.

The pond is frozen.

Maybe you should tell her to come across…..

Most of us do not know how to come across.

We are so concerned how we come across.

Other's opinions as to how they see us can be paralyzing. Well, privately, because we won't let anybody know. But there are those who see it readily, especially as you get older…..

How we appear is how we come across? A riddle?

If we worry about how we come across then maybe we can't come across as we really are… just who we wish to appear to be. Now maybe the other person is worried about how they come across? The blind leading the blind. Bet this happens more that we think.

Bet politicians are guilty. Bet that nations are guilty. Bet the State

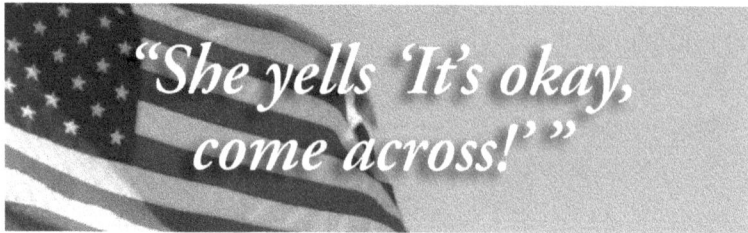

"She yells 'It's okay, come across!'"

Department is really worried about how we come across. Bet this worrying is all folly. I bet.

If we knew who we really were then we could act out of Truth. We could come across as genuine. When you know that someone means what he says you listen. There is no need for fine print. It is all spelled out in Truth. The Truth of a handshake. With a firm grip of course…. LOL.

Red Rover Come Over. An old child's game. Trying to get more people on your side.

What side do you want to be on?

There are only two. Sorry.

Good or bad.

Truth or lie.

Compassion or vanity.

Others or self.

Come a Cross?

Grand Wisdom Station

Up to a million commuters pass through Grand Central Station daily.

Over 90% have college degrees.

Their one-way commute can last 20 minutes or an hour and a half.

Over 20 million tourists visit it annually.

It's amazing… you gotta see it.

But everybody is in a hurry, running on the marble floors hoping their gate won't close on them. You don't learn much running, sweating, or worrying….

Grand Central Station is where time lapse video is an art form, a Picasso in motion. A virtual reality of everyone doing the Hustle in digital.

Destinations are critical to each commuter, coming and going. To work, to home…. To work, to home….

Home is where the love is. Family and children and friends.

Work is where you give your all to be of value and to be recognized in currency.

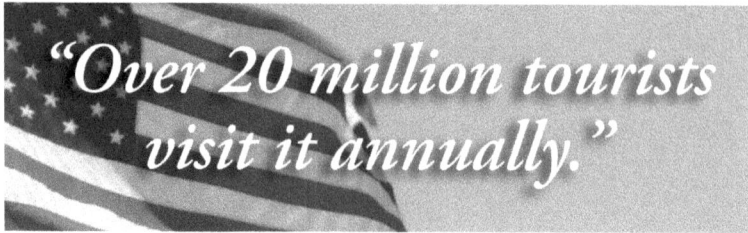

You have to think at work and expose your thinking to approval. You have to be careful to be seen thinking productively.

At home you are just asked to be there and offer example. To tuck in. To make sure all is good.

The days of the commuter become routine. And…. you better not miss the train or you will be late at your destination.

It is nice to have a destination of your choice. One wishes the destination to be both appreciative of you and comfortable with you. It is wise to know where you are going. Many don't.

Maybe we should rename Grand Central, to Grand Wisdom Station. Wisdom makes sure you choose the right train. One that takes you where you want to go…. Or where you need to go…..

Wisdom is found in experience…. And from having many years under your belt.

Generally you are slower and wrinklier when you get wise. The young don't look up to you unless they were brought up right. There is a sadness inside when what you have learned can't be shared…. Be put to better use. Maybe you should write… Get it?? LOL.

Wisdom is all about learning what is right. Accepting that evil is bad.

Accepting that on this planet evil is always deceitful. There is no easy way out.

Wisdom is also about the power of pure love.

It is about the power of Truth.

It is about the value of helping others.

It requires New Testimony.

All aboard??

Clap Discouraged

I hate canned laughter.

So many TV shows are phony as you know the laughter is recorded.

Shame on them.

In the old days there were these radio comedy shows that were great except for the canned laughter and applause. Now.... canned applause is a far greater sin......

When you just want to be you, and when something funny is said you want to be able to laugh. That is what is fun, being around friends and just laughing. Being spontaneously you. It is healthy.

I think the President likes it when they clap during his State Of The Union speech. OK, we know the other party abstains... LOL.. so funny... And then the Supreme Court is not allowed to clap.

How often do you get to clap in real life? We don't go to speeches. Hard to find moments when you feel good and you feel an enthusiasm kindled that forces your hands together in praise and approval?

It is also important for others to know what you stand for. Many will be silent but come up to you and thank you for clapping. Then you know you are right. Leaders can lead by clapping.

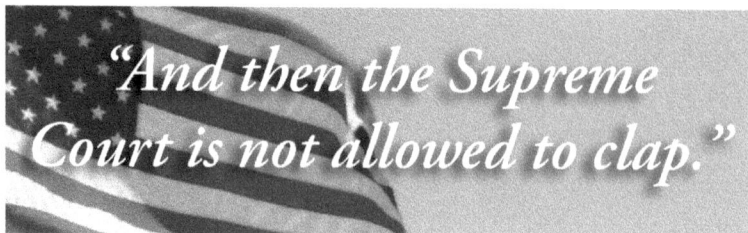

"And then the Supreme Court is not allowed to clap."

Of course, clapping at something that stinks or is evil makes you really stupid and accordingly dishonest to the others around you. Or, if they look up to you, you subvert them into a false identity.

So the moral of this story is that clapping should not be discouraged.

I think Jesus would have liked to hear more people clapping.

Then and today......

Hold your applause?

Ted?

Ford Tri-Motor

What is that noise outside?

No, not motorcycles… but it has a curious low-beat rumble.

I go outside and look up.

What in the world is that lumbering metal goose up there???

Big and slow.

Nothing stays up in the air going that slow!!

It's an old, real Ford Tri-Motor airplane from the 1920's!

Beautifully ugly.

Sure ain't no F35 Stealth Fighter.

Big old rotary engines thrumping to a steady beat.

There are tourists inside!!

You mean we trust something that was forged by hand before computers, before calculators?

Like it is a box with thick wings and folding chairs?

Why do we trust it?

"I go outside and look up."

Why is it making dozens of daily trips for all to experience?

The passengers sure dress differently.

The past has many beautiful secrets.

Beauty in forgotten forms.

Our history books are being purged of a lot of the beauty of Truth.

With a ride in the old Ford Tri…. Old is new…

Maybe we should try old values again too?

Hotel Colorado

Eagles soar high.............

Above the Rocky Mountains.

Why do they seem so happy so high?

Circling large swaths of land looking for prey.

Innocent prey.

Who wants to be taloned to death anyway?

Talons that hook deep into your soul and don't let go until you do....

In Hotel Colorado you can get high and soar in a lazy stupor, leaving responsibility and reality behind for a chosen time. You rise above others. Smiles become smirks in the talons of this eagle....

How to make things right is the real quest. Soaring feels really good. Free... be it above land or in the sea... Or family.... ???

Families need to be free of self. Time together just being free. Going up into mountains together. Sharing Truths. Just being together. Safe and with assuring glances always there. Dad. Mom. Daughter. Son. This is the real high. Not artificial. Bedrock quality time. Values winked. Closer to the Heaven. Coming down is full of joy.

"Above the Rocky Mountains."

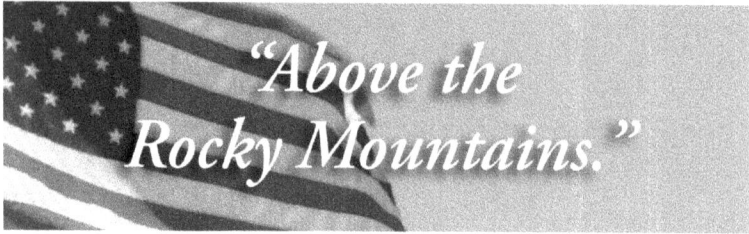

But coming down from an artificial high is filled with peril and pain and self-doubt. Maybe next time it will be better? Unseen talons taking you up again.

There are many ways to find altitude and not through attitude. Rocky Mountain high left for the eagle.

Make your Hotel Colorado a Cathedral.

In fact, walk into an old one in Europe. The vaulted ceilings beckon you to fly up to them. Made by hand in times when there was no science and there was no machine. Just a compelling vision and a gratitude to a Maker unseen. Look at the ceilings of the Sistine Chapel and soar in the unexplainable mystery of life and Hope. You lose contact with the ground for an unconscious moment.

You want to be a better person.

You wonder how you can get painted on a ceiling.

All it takes is to put your hand into that of a person in need.

You will feel the High.

We the Free

Surrounded by ocean.

We are set free from the worries of tyranny.

Few have a clue of what we had to do.

To create this paradise for you and for me.

Guns sounded.

Sailors "drownded".

In wars across the sea… for we the free.

Our borders are water.

Sometimes it is healthy to put on the other shoe.

Try someone else's to see how it fits and feels.

Suppose your neighbor just wanted to kill you.

And the border is just a line in the sand?

Oh, to be free of that chance.

But we are don't you see?

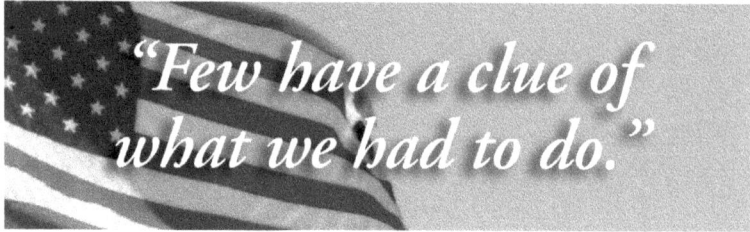

"Few have a clue of what we had to do."

We are not Israel.

It is just you and me.

Would you die to be free?

White Bread

This is not funny.

White bread is not funny.

White flour is not funny.

My doctor says to avoid.

So does my wife.

But it is in everything.

In fact, am told anything that is white is not good for me.

What about up in the clouds?

Grandpa Cuba

Families come from generations.

From what comes from the past.

We will never know when something said or done a long time ago was passed down through generations, if not centuries?

Fascinating thought we never think of.

Suppose some ancient ancestor 1,000 or 2,000 years ago had a good or bad characteristic and it was passed on over all the generations to you? Be really interesting to know. Has to be true... or at least a possibility?

Then we could blame some ancient being for it and have an excuse… or maybe able to thank that person…. If there is a heaven?…. Crazy notion isn't it?

Then there is us. Families are breaking up faster than you can blink. What will be passed on? New kids with new bruises. Their children receive the outfall, as will their kids…

How do we insure we are giving these kids better? It is up to us. A responsibility for sure. It requires an adult. It requires a good grandfather and grandmother.

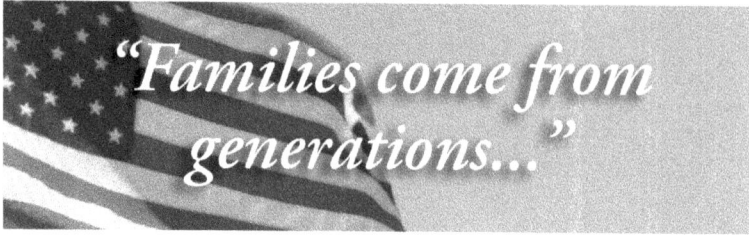

"Families come from generations..."

I know grandpa Cuba. He can't speak English so I really don't know him. He just got here. He actually gave his work life to the Cuban army. Go figure. His grandsons have turned out spectacularly. I can't imagine how unique they are.

Of course, there is still time for them to screw things up... but... they do have an iron mother who is on it all the time. Do not mess with this one! No playing for these boys. Work and work ethic is their spare time... as it should be. Somewhat akin to a boy growing up on a farm and always tending to something. From the heartland of America do come great young men.

Hard work anywhere makes the man.

Sadly, our Facebook entitled mindset is keeping too many from manhood.

Where do we find more Grandpa Cuba's?

We need men to fight Evil.

Millions of them.

If we are going to save our families and our country.

OMG.

Truthobabble

Truth is being debated everywhere all the time.

Everyone claims to know the Truth.

Politicians make it seem like their propriety knowledge.

Media savants then put their revealing spin on it.

And voila we have "truthobabble", "correctobabble", "psychobabble" and any other kind of "babble' you can create. It is "babble" chaos.

How can we find the Truth and help our kids know what it is?

We have this dilemma of each one of us having our interpretation of Truth which comes from many sources. We filter and decide and keep it private. Afraid to share for fear of being labeled or hurting someone else's feelings. Babble Prison.

What is correct?

Is there such a thing as correct?

Who gets to decide?

Who appoints who to determine what?

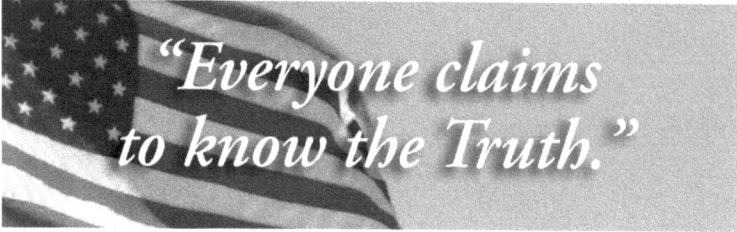
"Everyone claims to know the Truth."

We are going nuts trying to figure out rules. They are getting so detailed. And… there is always some group that will find a flaw in any line of any rule. Attorneys standing in line to help define cause and blame.

Does there not have to be a "yes" or a "no" most of the time, rather than a "maybe" and a debate on possible "feelings" impacted?

Is a feeling some sacrosanct final judge of a moment?

Do bad people have feelings we have to worry about?

If people choose to ignore our beliefs or rules are they better than us?

Are criminals protected by their legitimate feelings?

Is to disagree a sign of weakness or bias?

Thank God I can go to Google or Facebook to resolve my queries.

Going online for answers is so easy.

I just noticed that the Bible is online too.

OMG.

Die Young Old

I have a secret.

You never grow old.

You only look like you do!

Why don't old people tell the truth?

They walk around slow, talk a lot about health stuff, and kinda stick together in these communities where everybody looks alike.....

Well, if they are burdened with illness or bad medical issues, they are excused from this chapter. But... maybe not....

As time passes one sees more of what life does and does not have in store for you and for others. Wisdom about reality comes. Hopefully wisdom about how meaningful good is. A definition of good creates a life goal that is worthy. Hopefully, the subtle danger of evil becomes apparent. Hopefully, you choose to do something about it in your own world of family and friends.

You can be smart and young. You can remain young. In fact most do. Old people feel inside as young as they ever were, just smarter. When they meet old friends it is as if it was yesterday. It is amazing. It is

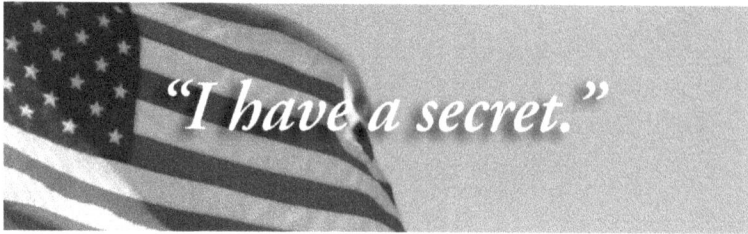
"I have a secret."

awesome (hate to use that word)... Nothing in the past changes...only in the future.... Meeting with old friends is like time travel. You share so much, especially the feelings of youth. Hard to explain, but it is beautiful.

Putting the body aside, there is just no reason to get old. Of course, you can choose to lament and act so. But that is the choice of the lazy.

Nothing makes one feel better or younger or more ageless than helping some other person. This is the most inescapable truth. Helping can be just a word of encouragement to solving a problem. Most people just want to know they are not alone. Be a "not-aloner"; one who can sense the negative drift in another and rush to their side. It is that easy. Wanna feel young?? .... Try it. In fact, if you open up your vision, you can do this until your last breath. You will always feel young.

Serve and you will be served.

When this Spirit enters you, your wrinkles will just not matter, just the smile on your soul.

There is a fountain of youth.

Look within.

The Camaraderie

It is the camaraderie.

One searches for truth and meaning under the guise of what makes one feel good.

There is entertainment, friendships, and all kinds of things which appear to be what life is

Often these are devoid of purpose, just activities that make one feel good in the moment.

But why I am here echoes deep within. Where do I make a difference? This is the man-quest. Women have birth and family. Man searches. Man succumbs to aloneness and journeys that lead nowhere. There is pain without purpose.

Military veterans come home and bring their private pain and surface smiles. Many have seen the belly of the beast. But it is the basic training and living together as brothers with tomorrow's uncertainties that forges a bond unimagined by civilians, by families even….Eating and sleeping often in extremely difficult circumstances. Never knowing the closeness of the unseen enemy or trap. There is always a mission and purpose to the next day… if it is just to take care and be with your buddies, your brothers in cammo.

"It is the camaraderie."

The meaning of your life is defined and private prides are worn.

Then you embark from the returning aircraft and receive the hugs of family. No one knows what your eyes have seen. They want you back as before. You are not the same. They can't get it….only your buddies who are spread far and wide from states to cemeteries.

Finding a job is often hard. Employers have no shared experience. They have no clue as to the disciplines and focus you have experienced. They are the amateurs in life, but don't know it. You have graduated, but don't know it.

Manhood comes from the camaraderie of combat; of getting close to evil. From being next to a buddy's last breath. From touching an artificial limb.

One had learned to communicate without sound. Eye contact rules...

Caring for a buddy more than one's self.

It's the damned camaraderie stupid.

Hire a veteran.

You owe it to yourself.

Fraternities

On college campuses they remain a bastion of the past.

Drinking establishments for students under the guise of a history of a refined club of students with a common purpose.

To exclude applicants not of like mind. Tricky terrain.

In today's Facebook world, the surface and how one wishes to appear becomes more important. Being able to manage one's image at an early age. Like minds are able to congregate and exalt sameness.

Upon exiting high school is the exciting independence of college. For many it is a serious journey with a secure future with an occupation in mind. But for many it is an intoxicating sojourn into freedom and beer.

Fraternity involvements are greater than ever as the need to belong has become more acute. You see… the insecurity created in our social network subculture has redefined the need of the individual to fit in. To be accepted and to have others aware of the same. It has always been this way, but now it is even more intense, fragile, and essential.

Fertile grounds for bigotry and waste and false prides.

Brotherhoods of frivolity.

Fraternities would be dynamic if each one had a real purpose, a real cause.

Take one, only one of the social causes, and solely commit a fraternity to it. You join if you want to make a difference. It could be a homeless shelter in your town or a food bank, or any non-profit, or create one... children's abuse, animal cruelty..... endless opportunities.

Just a thought.

After all, we are brothers??

Political Opportunity

I am not authorized to write about politics.

Want to lose a friend?

Something is confusing me.

Politics is spelled a lot like polite.

Maybe we should rename it.

Wouldn't it be great if a political opportunity became an opportunity to be polite?

Can you imagine a congress full of seated "politers"? How about a Senate?

We know that everyone on the Supreme Court is polite. Even attorneys are polite in those chambers.

Actually, everyone in church is not polite. They just talk behind backs…. Not to say there is not politics too. But most churches are great and special. They even try to be polite to the reformists…. LOL.

Politeness is often taken advantage of or disparaged as a weakness. You are told to be strong and forceful. You don't have to be polite with any form of evil.

"*I am not authorized to write about politics.*"

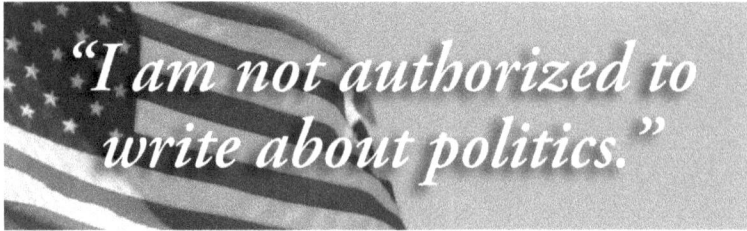

Politeness shows respect. We need to sit down and re-determine what/who we should be polite to. Of course, if you are a good person, being polite comes naturally. Probably means you had good parents who said "No" a lot... until you got it.

Now there are always opportunities to be polite if you are not lazy. Being polite makes the other person feel good too. And you will probably be closer to an agreement than you would have been otherwise.

Let's make a political opportunity one in which to be nice. Whereas today it is one of criticizing and destroying the opponent. I am not authorized to use the formal Party names that are donkeys and elephants. You would think they are cowboys running a steel cage match.

Who in the world wants to go for public office? It is more dangerous than ever. Misinformation is documented and celebrated. Wry political sarcasm trumps honesty and innocence.

Political comedy is the new serious.

I just don't understand those TV shows.

Abused political opportunities are the fertile soil of wars of all sorts.

Eventually reaching beyond our shores.

If we don't start being polite to one another, then there is no God.

All is lost.

Eye Peace

Hair piece.

Eyepiece.

Used to get close to something.

Part of a telescope.

How can you know about something if you can't get close… or at least closer?

It's all in the "optics" LOL.

We have been searching for peace for a long time. So many battles on so many fronts and so many of our young lost to the cause. Peace at all costs.

The stakes keep getting higher and higher. Now they are nuclear. And peace seems only to be had in endless debate and false reassurance. Diplomats of delay.

Peace at home, peace in the family, peace in the world, peace in the soul.

I would give up my life right here and now for peace. Would that not be great to do for our grandchildren and theirs?

"Part of a telescope."

So we truly need an eyepiece so we can see peace close up…

Readjust the focus.

Twist the lens to the right.

There it is…???

What is this Black Book?

The Bible.

The Bible??

Peace brother.

2 Parties

Who doesn't love a good party?

The best really are the spontaneous ones.

Last moment, impromptu. Fun.

What are you going to wear …if you have time…?

Where is it? I'm going anyway…

Then there are parties that are planned. Event driven. A little more serious. Can't tell if you are going to have as much fun…

Dancing? Drinking for sure? On the planned ones you are not sure of the invite list. But a party is a party.

You can be at a party and not feel it inside. Alcohol again helps. Maybe you don't know everybody… that's worse. Definitely a "where is the bar?" party.

Even for some parties you want to keep something in the car, cold beer in the trunk?? Just in case…. *pun intended*…

Ever been to a bad party? Couldn't wait to find a way out? Didn't feel comfortable? Yep, happens all the time, though few admit it. Artificial smiles, trivial conversation…..

"Who doesn't love a good party?"

Then in walks the person you have been looking for all your life! How to approach? What a shift in mood in an instant. LOL. Welcome to life.

Of course that person's head is lowered into a smart phone, texting. Texting who? Why? Wouldn't it be nice to have their number? To text that YOU are across the room!

Some people are blessed to always be having a party. The party is inside. When you are helping others, you see, you feel "gooder" than you ever did at any other kind of party.

It takes most a long time to get there.

But when that door opens the only bouncer is you.

The door on Sundays.

Drown It Out

Ever gone swimming way out far?

Like so far that you can't see land?

For 8-9 hours?

It gets creepy as you don't know where you might drown. And nobody will ever find you. Other than some big grey fish with lots of teeth.

Now if you have fins, a mask, a compass, and a swim buddy you have things to look at while passing the time. Lots of it. Kick, stroke, glide ad nauseam.

But by never quitting you get somewhere…

They didn't have waterproof ear buds back then. Of course then you wouldn't hear your buddy drowning or getting eaten.

I think there is a growing problem these days. The "ear-budders" have no clue what is going on around them. Hell, ISIS could shoot 20 people while they have "Happy" turned way up. I think there is a message here.

I see people walking, running, and working out on machines and treadmills totally absorbed in the "me" of music. It helps detach one from the discomfort and effort of exercise.

"Silence is deadly."

Symbolic of the seduction of all social networking? Artificial protection from reality if overused and abused?

Silence is deadly. That is if the outside world is silent to you. Your aural reverie sets you up for trouble……..

Of course, as with anything, moderation is a key to control and reasonable results. But who entertains moderation if pleasure or relief from discomfort is available?

And it is, if the ear buds are turned up….. Bee Gees? Maroon 5? … anyone?

You never know what they are listening to also….. they are drowning out reality.

It is like we are becoming experts at making reality go away.

The most unreal TV shows are the reality shows!!! LOL!! They contribute to the confusion of what reality is. Who defines reality?

Drown it out…! Drown it out…! Drown it out….! chant the worldwide billions of "ear-budders".

What is going to happen to the drowned when evil approaches and starts taking them one by one?

Drown it out with drinking, drown it out with uninformed thinking.

I am keeping my mask and fins at my side.

You ain't taking me down.

He Cried

He cried.

Why?

He had dropped something in front of a customer.

He was embarrassed. He is 16. He is also brilliant.

It terrified me when I heard the story.

Our "looking-downers", our "ear-budders", our "whateverers", are becoming a generation with diminished social skills other than when on their "social networks".

The days of "yes maam" and "yes sir" are now ancient relics of a culture stronger than we thought. The handshake with direct eye contact has meaning only to a stalwart few.

Young kids need social, real interpersonal skills and confidence when with peers and those in authority. They are not getting it from their cell phones and Facebook. They are invisibly being conditioned to becoming insecure.

In the real world, in the real moment decisions have to be reflexive and instant. No time to look down. Only experience drives success. It is our

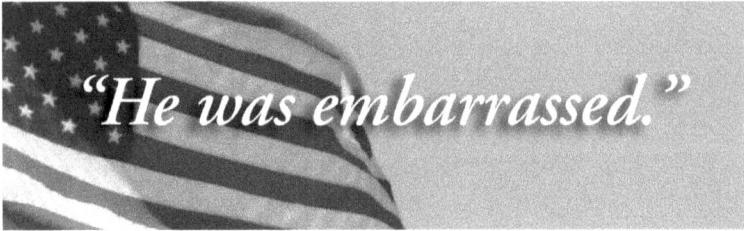

"He was embarrassed."

instant reaction that defines us. That gives a glimpse into who we might be. And we are judged accordingly.

If you have a giving heart, no, better put, a serving heart… you will be pulled out of disaster. You will become proud and others will feel comfortable around you. And you will feel it.

I feel so much more insecurity and concurrent insincerity all around these days as people talk with cliché and universal response words that they can hide behind. "Howya doing?", "What's up?", "No problem!", "No worries.", "Whatever."…. And the LOL, BFF, OMG acronyms are endless. Fascinating assault on Our Webster Dictionary (OWD?)… LOL.

But these are threatening the core strengths of our culture.

Distancing themselves so easily from responsibility and accountability.

Maybe even God.

So much will be lost before it is too late.

Then we will cry.

Whatever.

Feeling Good

HOWZIT GOIN?

Why?

Do you really care when you throw out that reflexive remark?

Shows me more about your insecurity rather than genuine concern.

I feel absolutely fabulous.

Do you?

There is nothing, absolutely nothing better than feeling good. Ask people what makes them feel good and you will get the "goodest" answers in the universe and few are the same. Most answers will talk about life's pleasures… you know …wine, women, and song… or cars, sports, vacations, weddings, kids, and family just for starters.

And it is true they give you a taste of what feeling good is all about. Throw in laughter. Throw in happy tears…. We both could keep going and have a lot of fun. Fun works too.

Feeling bad is no good. It shows, and the energy we throw out is not pleasant to anyone near or dear. Definitely avoid people who are feeling bad. However, if we could feel what makes the person feel bad we might

"I feel absolutely fabulous."

be able to help. But is the possibility of rejection worth it?

Good people can feel bad. Bad people can feel good. Like the terrorist who feels good giving up his life in terrifying the innocent.

When we are scared about something we might withdraw or seek protection. If we don't then we are foolish.

When your time is up, it just is. It is your choice to feel good up until that moment. But that often means a major change. Where self is just no longer an obsession. In the simple act of reversal, in just caring for others you transcend all earthly pain. You are too busy doing good which just makes you feel good.

Look over your shoulder and see lines of people you have helped.

You will feel blessed.

What a special feeling.

Truly amazing... even awesome.....

Feeling good.

A Spade

A spade is a spade is a spade.

Doesn't that mean that nothing is no more than what it is??

It doesn't mean that it is a riddle or has other meanings. It just means that black is black and white is white.

But we can no longer call a spade a spade. Liberals call it one thing and conservatives another. Go figure.

Conservatives say it is a tool that makes entry into a plot of ground and throws the last spadeful on the grave.

Liberals say it is a process of protecting man from having too many pets… and they spell it different. They like neutering everything with academic acclaim.

Therein lays our quandary. And therein lays our defeat in the next war. It is called the "dithering spade" or Grey Tongue Disease, GTD. We debate the obvious and decide nothing. Media gobbles up the disagreement and confusion creates the new grey.

If your fellow citizen is beheaded, I don't think any letter to the NY Times will make a difference. People don't desist from being bad just

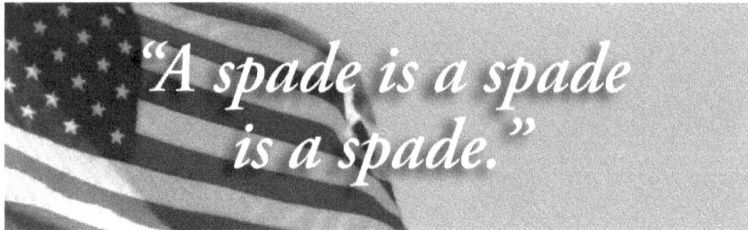

because you say it is wrong. They will reconsider their choices if there is real threat of death, economic and mortal. Shoot some first, then ask questions… as the old expression goes.

Why are we so afraid to call a spade a spade? Why have we taken the spades out of our history books? Why are we afraid to use the color black? Why is white now problematic?

Language is becoming vague. Phrases are beginning to mean nothing. We are becoming a nation of insecurities. Afraid to upset anyone. Afraid to be unique. Afraid to have values.

Oh my goodness, what has happened?

Time to gather in small groups with our spades.

And all chant "A spade is a spade is a spade".

Shuffle the deck.

Something Fishy

Sometimes something just feels not right.

Premonition?

Or just a private suspicion that something is fishy….

Feel that way about the world?

There is so much poverty and violence and it is now the 21st century! We have put man on the moon and an apple on our wrist. What gives?

The fishing boat goes out into the ocean and brings back a magnificent catch. Offloads and gets a great price for the 5,000 lbs. of tuna. The Japanese really pay for quality tuna. But the boat smells fishy. Really hard to get that smell out. You could if you wanted to…..

Why in the USA are there so many poor? We can understand Africa and the Middle East… but the USA?

Admittedly we have been nourishing an entitlement subculture, but there is more to it than that.

The rich are getting richer they say… Our financial institutions have fees on transactions that insure few walk away with more. Why does a hedge fund manager or even broker get paid so much for phone calls

"Sometimes something just feels not right."

promoting us gambling on "sure" things? The art of the deal?

Workers still provide the product and seldom share in these profits. Something is fishy. We are a nation, a democracy that is a family of the Constitution of fairness and justice. The rich really can afford to do with less. They would still be creative and productive with half their incomes.

There are companies that truly respect the employee and really take care of them. Unions aren't needed when there is honesty and true appreciation of the contribution every employee makes.

We have tiered ourselves into inefficient structured bureaucracies where supervisor reports to supervisor who reports to supervisor. Fertile ground for politics??

How often does the CEO go into his trenches and shake the hands of the supervised?

Who praises whom and how… and when??

In WWII factories sprang up all across the nation to produce war materials. 500 bombers a day. And we felt good. And most everyone had an honest job.

There was no money being skimmed by financial fishermen….

Values were different then. That war had to be won. We are the beneficiaries. Yet we have also enabled the next war by not keeping our values intact

Values in the boardroom and values in the home.

Have we created the greatest Ponzi scheme of them all?

Pretending we are found when we are lost?

Something is fishy.

I sure love the Swan River Fish Restaurant across the street.

Unequal Equals

All men were created equal as affirmed by us on July 4, 1776.

It is easy to say.

But we know there are so many people who do not deserve this consideration.

Even some who should just be shot.

Everyone has their own list.

This "equal" stuff is a little antiquated. People have yachts and fly around in private jets and others miss payments on their car. For the most part those at the bottom work harder than those on the top.

Of course you can get ahead with hard work and commitment. But those opportunities are getting more elusive.

We may have developed a systemic inequality where a significant percent are guaranteed relative poverty, or certainly limited access to the middle class. And where the middle class can only look up and hope…..

Politicians and preachers today tell us we are all equal….. but how?

"Even some who should just be shot."

Where is the leader who can bring us together both morally and "opportunity-ally" *(like the new word?)*

A leader who can remold bureaucracy to serve rather than self-administer. Who can make bonuses really taxable? Who can transparently attack inefficiency and inequality? Who can redefine entitlement in a way that is honest and focused on the real needy, not on those who know how to play the system? Laziness can no longer be protected by the system.

You can't make decisions behind a desk. You can't make decisions based upon layers of approvals. Someone must look someone in the eye and make a judgment… Someone must accept responsibility for a decision. It must no longer be easy to pass the buck. Delay because of administrative requirements is a scam.

July 4, 1776 was meant to make us honest and equal. Lives were lost fighting for this nation to be free. In every war. Now we are losing more lives from inequality than war...

"We hold these truths to be self-evident, that *all men are created equal*, that they are endowed by their Creator with certain unalienable Rights…."

Have we lost our way?

Is inequality institutionalized?

"Creator?"

You kidding me??

Blowing In The Wind

The melody echoes in my head.

Where are the answers to life?

What in the world are we?

What are we supposed to be doing?

What is time?

What should I do with it?

What is love?

Why does it keep interrupting?

What is family?

Who are children?

Where did an orchid come from?

Why are puppies so pure?

Why is good so beautiful?

Why do we turn away?

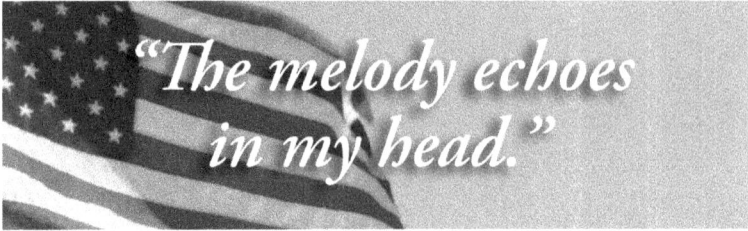

> "The melody echoes in my head."

What is peace?

Do tears make peace?

Who gets to be evil?

Who gets to kill?

Who cleans up?

Who forgives?

Why?

Bad Dog

You ain't nothing but a hound dog.

You ain't nothing but a "bad dog".

You bark all the time.

You are always dirty.

You lick too much and hang around with the wrong crowd. When they run somewhere you are right in the middle of the pack. Dachshund, Dalmatian, or Dane it doesn't matter who you breed with. You are always breeding, or trying to.

It's not that pleasant seeing you frolicking that way in public all the time. But for the most part you like one another regardless of what you look like … purebred or crazy mix. I have yet to see a Dane-Dachshund mix. Maybe on German Google??

Dogs get called bad all the time. "Bad Dog" for peeing on the carpet. "Bad Dog" for not understanding what you are trying to tell him. They don't get it until you raise the newspaper. That is black and white to them! (*pun intended*).

Golden Retrievers are the only breed that is perfect. They are the right

size, the right color, the right shape, just right all around. They are best when by themselves, loving their family and not having to get involved with the world. Some say it is not right to expose them to the outside world. They say they can't handle the Truth. Sounds ridiculous.

Then there are some really ugly dogs out there. My college mascot was as ugly as they get. Mascots were meant to fight one another.

The problem with all of this is that there is no such thing as a bad dog.

All dogs are good.

All dogs are fantastic if they are treated with love.

My God do they redefine trust. Even bad people are nice to their dogs, except really bad people. Your dog looks into your eyes with trust and for answers. Total friendship. But…. you have to earn it the hard way by always being consistent in how you show your love.

That is all our children ask of us. But we are treating them not as nice as our dogs. Their fathers are moving out and away in greater and greater numbers. Our children are becoming like lost dogs in the social networks of fickle love. Trying to find nourishment from scraps of conversation. While overwrought and overworked moms fight on…

There is no such thing as a bad kid.

When we don't fully protect and teach it the Truth from infancy the odds are against it.

Puppy love it is called.

South Pole

The North Pole is cold and barren.

The ocean below is 13,000 feet deep.

The South Pole is really cold and barren.

It has mountains.

You don't want to live there.

You can only stay warm at the North Pole in a nuclear submarine.

You can stay warm at the South Pole in the McMurdo Sound Station, Antarctica.

Life is cruel at the poles.

Now in between the water is warm and the weather is good, though a little hot at the equator.

There is only so far north you can go and there is only so far south you can go. Your choice. In either case these extremes do not offer safe haven.

Maybe there is an analogy between the left and the right?

It sure seems like we are all trying to pick a pole to live on. Democrat or Republican. Polarized. Frozen in time. Cold to reason. Cold to compromise. Cold to agreement. Cold to love.

"You don't want to live there."

The world is the same. Extremes fighting normality. Evil basking in the void of polarizations. Evil cannot be brought to justice if those who are good are not united.

God didn't create us to live on the poles.... Our bodies may still be in the USA but our politics are way out there in accusation land. Senate or Congress, it is freezing in there. So many well intentioned corrupted by the winds of power and money swirling in confusing vortexes across their chambers. A maelstrom of moral chaos. It is becoming a moral issue as it is stimulating injustice to all.

Maybe this is just life as it is. Our planet is no more than it is. The poles couldn't be further away.

But it is all so awesome. From sub-atomic particles to the stars in the sky. From the pulse of our being to the compassion in our heart.

It is time to write down what is valuable to us.

Like our forefathers on July 4, 1776.

United we stand.

Divided we fall.

Let's Pretend

Let's pretend.

Let's pretend you are rich.

Let's pretend you have great hair.

Let's pretend you can have any car you want.

Let's pretend you have a great personality.

Let's pretend you really know how to dress.

Let's pretend all heads turn when you enter the room.

Let's pretend everybody likes you.

Let's pretend there is no selfishness.

Let's pretend there is no injustice.

Let's pretend everyone is equal.

Let's pretend there is no evil.

Let's pretend there are no suicide-bombers.

Let's pretend there is no corruption.

"*Let's pretend you are rich.*"

Let's pretend there is no politics.

Let's pretend there is no child abuse.

Let's pretend there is no women's abuse.

Let's pretend there is no hunger.

Let's pretend that all of the above are not true.

Let's pretend we know what we are doing.

Let's pretend there is no God.

Are we living under false pretenses?

Universe Within

Ever been outside on a dark clear night and look up?

Stunned by the beauty of the stars.

Actually overwhelmed when trying to understand it so you just look and say… "Aren't those stars beautiful?" And you leave it at that… other than commenting to a friend how beautiful the sky was last night…..

Of course you could have taken the hand of a child and walked up the hill and looked at the heavens together. Trying to explain the magic enormity of it all. That they can't finish counting the stars as more keep appearing with better telescopes aboard spacecraft.

How do you explain it? Do you even try? Does the child not deserve the Truth? Are you able to explain the Truth when scientists can't? Black holes swallowing universes. Crazy, absolutely crazy stuff going on above us all the time… crazy.

OK, we will send Orion and 3 men to Mars and that will explain everything. I bet their telescope will see further beyond and our imaginations will be in awe again. The craziness will just increase.

There was a science fiction movie a while ago about a fantastic voyage through the arteries and veins of man. In some way, this gave one a

view into the amazing complexity of the human body. We take so much for granted as we go about our busyness and days and needs and entertainment.

Seldom pausing to question how our organs and brain and blood and skin is made of cells which are made of atomic particles which are made of subatomic particles which are made of some crazy particles called quarks, leptons, and bosons which may have something to do with force or something....

So whether we look up, down, or in we cannot comprehend who we are or where we are.

How did this all happen? Beats me. Science says it just happened. Some Big Bang theory or whatever. Does that answer all?? Not in the slightest. Nor does this discredit the awesome art of science which continues to reveal the unlimited potential of man.

But how can we exist without knowing where we came from? To not really fully understand existence. We just keep on keepin' on.

There is another world further deep within that explains it for me. Soul stuff. All falls into place if one accepts God as a reality. That Creation happened.... as we are told in those stories that have been handed down. They are easy to discredit, but what is the point when they provide the only remaining logical answer to us?

We are a beautiful creation with unlimited potential to do good and evil.

We are our own mystery with complexities greater than the heavens.

Emotions and gifts inexplicable.

It is our choice to believe or not.

But if you do, your potential explodes.

You will see potential acts of kindness you never could before.

You can find real joy.

Now what kind of particles are they made of???

Deconstruction

Taking things apart...

That's what children do when left alone.

After the Civil War the reconstruction was deconstructed and nothing happened with civil rights. Nothing.

It takes too much toil and blood to build something good. Think of the former cities in the Middle East today. Think of the World Trade Center. Think of all the men who built them. The hours and years they spent in tremendous toil and planning. Bombs and missiles create rubble in minutes. Like children.

But try and think philosophically. Deeper. What is the root cause of the deconstruction of good? Think of all the good man has accomplished, and by good people doing good for others..... Think of parents who love their children and treat them with real respect by disciplining them.

By saying "No" even when it hurts. Parents who know the values that were passed down by generations. Forging offspring who would make good lives and raise their children correctly.... Like in the past.

Think of schools which used to teach right and wrong.

"That's what children do when left alone."

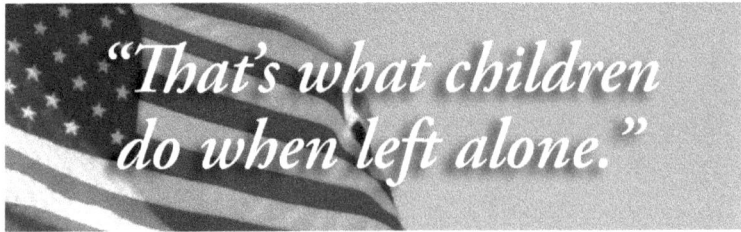

Our whole value system is under attack and we laugh it off. We are allowing our liberties to be liberated from us by those who yell from the fringes. The media is neutering our values.

The keyboards of social networks are deconstructing our family traditions. Bureaucracies are so ponderous that they deconstruct the truth with volumes of legalistic fine print. Everyone's ass is covered but yours.

Values are what you die for. Values are only about what is good. It is simple. All you have to do is state what is good and then stand for it. Do not be swayed by the doubts of others.

If you don't really stand for something then you are a nobody; truly everything you don't want or need to be. Your choice.

You can study religion. Religion can be boring and hypocritical if you let it. It is the spirit within religion and you that comes from God. This Spirit is Holy. You can't find it in all the wrong places… Duuhh.

I beg you to let go of preconceived notions about religion and move beyond conventional prejudice. Go to as many churches as you can until you find one which resonates, where what you hear feels good inside. I have been to 100's and only a few were right. But when they are, wow. You know you are somewhere special… and different.

Let that spirit deep within you keep you going.

Don't quit.

Or you will never know who you could have been.

Sure You Can

I don't know classical music at all.

I remember the Lone Ranger radio show and its William Tell Overture…. That's sadly it.

The Everly Brothers, the Kingston Trio, and the Beatles killed any chance of classical surviving, much less opera. No, not Oprah dummy…..

Yet people in large quantities have never let go of the classical. It is a pure art form in music…. And not the Picasso-ization of popular music.

We watch The Voice and these struggling vocalists make it to national TV and its grand rejections to find the winner. Some came back from prior years because a Pharrell Williams, or Blake Shelton etc…. may have said "Sure you can". Go back and work harder.

We all need to hear "Sure you can." more often and we desperately need to encourage others the same way.

Sure you can get that job.

Sure you can feel better.

Sure you can climb that mountain.

"Sure you can get that job."

Sure you can have better manners....

Let's see which of us can make the longest list of "Sure You Can's."

I say to all you young wannabe SEALs.... Sure You Can!

If you shook hands with every new graduate of BUDS *(Basic Underwater Demolition Seal)* school... you would say he looks just like me... or did several years ago... a scrawny kid with pimples....

You see, you have to work very hard and long to condition yourself to achieve all goals. Every real rich person was poor once.

Nothing of value is effort free.

It is the *not giving up spirit* in spite of the "it's not worth it" wall that everyone faces. Quitting just takes saying "I quit"... "This is not for me." and ringing life's bell.

Yet one failure can lead to a different success. It is all a question of attitude, spirit, and sense of humor. Sure you can.

Someone on the piano this morning at church was playing some classical piece. I thought this guy is real good. A student? I looked at the program. *Impromptu No. 4 G flat major by Franz Schubert.* Now this is the real deal folks. I strained to see the pianist. A young, neat looking, black man.

All I could think was "Sure You Can.".

He has already played in Carnegie Hall.

Wow, I got to hear him play today.

"Sure you can."

Seriously?

There is no reason to take anything seriously.

Anything serious can be debated as to its real seriousness.

In the process the serious is diluted and the insignificant exalted.

So we have all these serious issues trying to reach the government agenda but are so dissected by media and politics that they become emotional then boring.

Seriously?

This word is an expression of weakness by many. It is just one word, but with a question mark at the end, the responder is intimating that it is not serious. Well, it doesn't take a genius to know when someone or something is serious.

"Seriously?" falls into the category of "awesome" and "whatever". The new vocabulary of mediocrity and social network identity crisis.

I come back real quick and real hard. YES, I am serious! And here is why… with an intense and complex retort.

We just have to find a way to take things more seriously. The world is in political and moral chaos. We had better face up to it and make some

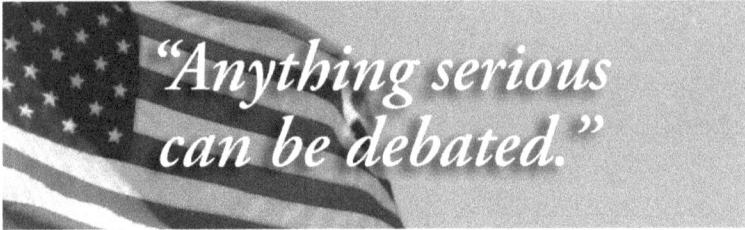
"Anything serious can be debated."

hard choices rather than hoping it will go away… or get better over time.

WWII must not be forgotten. We dithered and the war doubled in human and dollar cost. We kept saying "seriously?" to ourselves while Auschwitz was being built and soldiers marched on borders. Evil is real. Proven time and time again.

Don't we get it???

Life is serious.

Abuse is serious.

Freedom is serious.

Fairness is serious.

Marriage is serious.

Compassion is serious.

Generosity is serious.

Every human being can have value.

Seriously?

UnTwo

It takes two to tango.

I wish we could dance.

You know, her arm around his shoulder.

His arm around her waist.

They spin out in the tango's seduction of movement and agreement.

Delicate balance with energy and art to the music which binds.

But… you have to embrace in the process…..

Doctors and patients.

Fathers and sons.

Congress and Senate.

Democrats and Republicans.

Husbands and wives.

But what if we don't learn how to dance?

We will be dancing the dance of chaos and not know it. Well, we are.
Heads down into the assurances of texting. Thinking we are secure.

"It takes two to tango."

Take away the phones. Look up finally and it may be too late. You thought you only needed dark to dance in. Wrong. The real dance is in the light … looking up.

The dance of Truth, the dance of Caring, the dance of Love.

The dance with God.

There is no other dance that doesn't end.

You need His dance instructors.

They can be found coming and going from churches.

Pure Water

The field is flooded.

It must be drained.

Then there is drought.

Again nothing can grow.

Rains come.

The soil is fertilized.

Drop a seed and food is born.

Amazing.

Right soil and more and more seeds can be planted. Many, many more mouths can be fed. Truth can spread.

It is a simple process that has existed for thousands of years and millions of people. If you don't take care of the land it cannot take care of you.

Our souls are the same. But we all act as if we don't care. Too many important things to do now rather than plan for the future and the cards it may deal. Now. Me. Not Thee.

No seeds in the soil. Seeds not growing. In us.

"The field is flooded..."

Should we all not sow seeds? Good values need to be sown. Remember who sowed yours?

Evil is growing again because we haven't fertilized our soils. We are weak with conviction. We are not building values in our young. We are yielding to the toxins of sensitivities and self.

We only come together in crisis. And even now as new crisis-events are played out in the news we cannot stand back and see the big picture. We are losing and don't see it. There is too much vibrant color to distract the senses on the screens. Too many commercials to interrupt thought.

How do we reclaim the land?

We have bottled all our waters.

Pure water in plastic.

Something is missing.

We have bottled the water to the soul.

Something is missing.

Who will hold the cup up to His parched lips?

Natural Disaster

Tornado.

Tsunami.

Flood.

Plane crash.

Beheadings.

Evil.

Things happen that are out of our control. Good and bad things. But we remember and recoil at the bad things. The bigger question is where is the line between natural disaster and disaster we create?

Most would argue that we don't create "disasters" only nature does? Go to the dictionary. Is a hit-and-run a disaster? Sure is to the family of the deceased. Oh, it was a drunk… Horrible, but it was a drunk. Or his mind was on something else, speeding, texting. Horrible and sad but we understand.....

The courts are fair for the impaired. What is impaired? Anyone responsible?

"Tornado."

Is it a disaster when to a parent the child says "whatever"? Is this a domestic disaster? Is it natural? The answer lies seeded in the child who has become indulgent and corrupted by lack of discipline and by the freedoms of social networks. A technically induced disaster?

But we do have choice?

Is to make the wrong choice a natural disaster?

When are we going to own up to the fact that we are our own ticking natural disaster? We are a part of nature?

We can only be ready if we know the meaning of true love.

The rescue crews have to put recovering the bodies above their own safety.

We can only rescue our family or our country if we put them above ourselves.

"Greater love hath no man than to lay down his life for another."

A natural disaster can come at any time.

Good Friday??

DawnRise

"Oh say can you see by the dawn's early light?"

When you open your eyes and see the first light of the morning….. is there a storm, or rain, or clouds, or sun??

Dawn is a joy in either case.

You are alive and still capable of making another difference.

Can you see this?

Bringing light to anything, much less Earth, is revealing and allows one to see the path. It is easier to choose a path in the light than in the darkness.

At home there are light switches and lamps. Outside the headlights or flashlight or municipal lighting….. No light and you break your ankle and fall down. Old people break hips.

When sun sets one prepares for darkness. In darkness the pawns of evil come out. We lock our front doors.

There is darkness during the days …these days. Travel with caution and know where you are going. There are countries to avoid. Where people live in fear and darkness 24/7.

"Oh say can you see?"

Ignorance is darkness also. Ignorance creates insecurity. We can live in our own private darkness.

Truth is the light of the world. Truth is the light of our futures. Without Truth all is in vain. Truth is worth fighting for, even if it is our Truth versus their truth…. We need to control the switch not them. ISIS is not the truth, their ideology is its own cancer. Metastasizing as we allow them switch access. A darkness we choose not to acknowledge.

The world has so many areas of darkness.

Too many?

Why can't the world unite against the darknesses?

Is it time for a new sunrise within us?

Sonrise?

Easter?

Me Worry?

What... me worry?

Get outta here...

What is there to worry about other than my bills, my taxes, my wife, my kids, my job, my vacation, my car, my hair, my mirror?

Come on... "What? Me worry?"

Let everyone else do all the worrying. That is why we elect officials and presidents. I should only have to worry if there is enough beer in the refrigerator.

Anyway, all I have to do is look down and see who just sent me a text. I can ask them if they are worried. No, not as long as we are texting. There are just no worries.

In fact, that is even the reply of the waiter when you ask for your pizza with extra cheese. He says "no worries" and your pizza comes out as if there never was a conversation.

Hey, the Pope got his pizza delivered with extra cheese too....

So, no matter where you are there is little left to worry about as reassurances are always immediately available.

Deep down inside where the Truth lies, there are simmerings of concern.

"What.. me worry?"

The world ain't right. Too much hunger, abuse, and violence...... what can one person do anyway?

The answer is that 1 million or 50 million or 200 million little individuals become big if they embrace the same Truths. But they don't want to. Like babies getting their way. The politicians ain't helpin' either. Nor their TV media partners, nor the finger pounders on the social networks. Nobody is helping.

It is time to stop worrying.

A worry takes up time. It distracts one from purpose and decision.

Our kids need to see us solving problems, not talking about them. It is time for us to gather at the dinner table and talk about the good done of the day. How it was accomplished. What hurdles were overcome. Then a prayer together, holding hands... while Norman Rockwell paints.....

I will not worry if you will not worry.

Love doesn't worry.

Lovers don't worry.

That's the Truth.

Tooth Fairy

Dad tied the string to the door knob, then slammed the door.

Tooth came right out.

Shortly thereafter mom and I put the tooth under my pillow with a wish.

I forget what I wished, but am sure it came true.

It was almost something to look forward to.

Today I had some gum surgery and some bone grafting on my front tooth. Seemed the implant had a little infection. Evil stuff inside.

Now my dentist has pretty eyes, lovely personality, and a dedication to helping others. We can't help others if she can't help us. Crazy unpleasant stuff. Scraping, pushing, cutting, spreading, sewing. Very intimate. In fact what is more intimate?

There is a bond of trust as one's mouth opens to receive the needle and knife unlike any other kind of surgery. It is in your head!

How do they do it day after day? Where is the glamor in medicine? Same rooms every day. Patients come and go, you still do the same thing. You get good at it. Doing the same thing. That is how one

"Dad tied the string to the door knob."

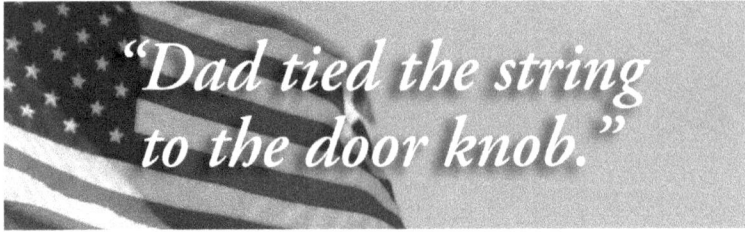

becomes a professional, how one gets good at any job. She was crazy good.

But there is a life lesson here.

Trust is key to success. How do you trust someone you know is going to bring you pain? You just do it. You can't count on anyone else's word other than your own. Your heart has to say "just do it".

How can you trust a God you can't see?

Only in good can you find God. You have to do good to believe that good is better than evil. You have to do it day after day just like the surgeon. You have to do it every day until you die. Then the mystery of everything will be understood.

It's kind of like tying a string to the ego and having your dad shut the door.

It really only hurts for a little while and then you can be proud of your smile regardless.

To some their dad is God.

Harp Sanitizer

What gives?

Everywhere you go there is sanitizer lotions, soaps, wipes…Yuck.

Has Howie Mandel frightened everybody?

There are germs everywhere.

Doorknobs, turn indicators, tooth brushes, pill bottles, refrigerator doors, window latches, scissors, watches….

There must be an exploding market for sanitizer specific task items… Holy Moly Wall Street… get going….

What happens in the grocery store? Are the shopping carts sanitized… they don't look that clean... Should we carry florescent lights to see if germs are alive? What about the bakery counter? Any germ fingerprints? This is so fun thinking about all the endless possibilities.

How did we survive with vigor to today… in the year 2015?

While we obsess about germs we turn away from spiritual germs. Germs that attack the soul. Germs that affect rational thinking.

The internet provides instant access to evil. Social networks need

"There are germs everywhere."

sanitizing? Would this be an attack on freedom of speech? Do germs have rights?

When an adult plants a bad-word-germ in a child it is too late. Don't we get it?

Good, thoughtful behavior and thinking is required by all. Especially when the infectious diseases from the Middle East are not being cured. A sanitizer no longer has any effect. Only a strong antibiotic that has not been field tested yet.

Looks like our sanitizers are not working on Putin and definitely not on Kim Jung Un. Maybe it is time for some new formulas? Nuclear worked the last time... Just kidding...

Is this just happening on Earth?

Do you think it is spreading to heaven?

Will you have to bring up some harp sanitizer?

OMG.

Good 2.0

Remember the first time you heard the word good?

When your mom said "good girl" or "good boy"?

Or "You did good!"

What is it about this word that feels good… deep within…making you smile deep inside…. Maybe your first exposure to pride…. And maybe even humility as a small ripple of embarrassment is first felt…. Funny, all this about 4 letters….

Then there is the person who tells you that you are no good. Or an employer who says look elsewhere. Or a spouse who says I'm leaving…. Times when one does not feel good. Of course on the battlefields of life where danger and evil conspire, you can get feelings that are not good….

But the first time you heard "good" it was about right and wrong. It defined how you should judge things in the future. Good and bad labels made things simple. But only if they were consistent. No shades of grey.

Firm foundations are based on strong ideals and values. These can only come from a strong home and parent. From poverty come the strongest leaders because they know the value of good and bad. Good and bad

"Good is felt by all."

effort. Good and bad character. Good and bad money. Good and bad love. Put them in college and they study.

Good is felt by all. Missed by many and undervalued by most. Doing good, pursuing good leaves no regrets.

You know when you do good.

You just know.

It is a Truth.

Really a most unusual word.

Only four letters.

Two consonants and two vowels.

Even more amazing is what's left if your remove one vowel.

OMG.

Who Art

There is a famous British band "The Who". They are celebrating their 50th Anniversary in a 2015 world tour. Go figure? Who lasts that long? *(note pun)*

Last year was the 50th anniversary of my BUDS class. Go figure. Who lasts that long? Nine were left for this reunion.

Who is a big question these days. Who else is going to last to their 50th reunion of whatever?

Who you are is more important. Have you made choices that will allow you to make a 50th? Think of all the bad choices one can make. Many, many shorten life. More bad choices than good ones will increase the odds of you dying younger and therefore with fewer wrinkles.

I like my wrinkles. They are badges of knowledge. Whether of wisdom is for you to decide.

Old people can wink more. We wink to older peers who also know. It is the "get it?" wink. It's great to be able to communicate with others so much more effectively. Actually a wink is an affirmation of agreement without dozens of lawyers providing fine print clarity.

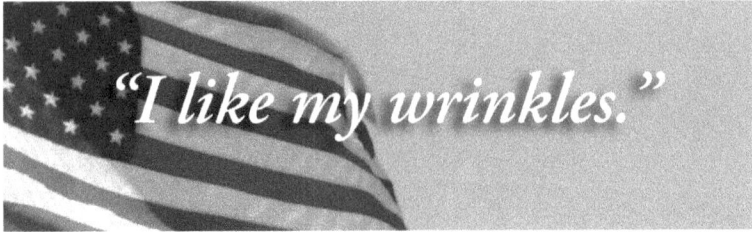

"I like my wrinkles."

Will you be remembered for the "Who" of you. What Who? We have surface Who's which we construct for others to see and like. We spend a lot of time on appearance. Clothes, beauty, possessions, money all contribute to that Who.

But the inner Who is who we are. The hidden who. When your heart is hidden behind the walls of insecurity no one can really know you. Hearts on the sleeve expose our reality. Do we have compassion? Do we care for others? You can't hide that. And you shouldn't. It is what life is really all about. And should be what it is only about.

Doing good.

Is your Who good?

Do you like your Who?

Does everybody else?

Does your Father?

Who art..........

Red

Red is a stripe on our flag.

Red stands for valor and bravery.

On those fields of blood.

Red is a dramatic favorite of women.

Valentines are red.

Red switches connote danger and emergency.

Cardinals that fly and pray are red.

Red at night sailor's delight.

We go through life searching for meaning. Because it is so elusive and quixotic we often just give up and have another glass of wine. Laughter and fun seem to have meaning… of course, depending on what kind…

But as we have explored from every angle in these books we all come back to the same place. That doing good is better than doing bad. That being unselfish is better than being selfish. It is pretty plain and simple if we are honest with ourselves.

Putting a smile on the face of another is our smile inside. Serving

"Valentines are red."

someone else is the ultimate sport.

We ask ourselves where to go to find out how to get there.

Who can we go talk to?

The answer, like it or not, lays in an old Black Book.

You can talk to Him.

If you can read Red Print.

OMG.

EPILOGUE

I have been blessed with a journey that has not seen the real poverty or felt the real pain of the majority. Please don't judge me by the immaterial, much less the material. I was born in Bronxville, NY in 1940. Grew up in Louisville and St Louis. Graduated from Yale and went into the Navy. I had the great honor of fulfilling my dream to become a Frogman. I graduated from BUDS Class 31E, Basic Underwater Demolition/Seal School. I was an officer in Underwater Demolition Team 21 which became Seal Team 4 in 1984. I had the honor of recovering several spacecraft, including Gemini 6/7 & AS-201, the very first Apollo Spacecraft to go into space. Wow, did I luck out. Then I spent 40 years in women's retail, in various department stores. Even a year at the World Wrestling Federation... go figure?

I have two great daughters and two grandchildren who have just discovered the water and facemasks. My wife has created probably the #1 women's accessory store in the country as evidenced by how much she is copied. Therein I work and report to her... No comment. LOL.

As you can tell by reading between the lines there is a spiritual side to my journey. Kind of covert as I just want to make a difference unseen.

God Bless You All... Happy Trails.

IN THE WORDS OF OTHERS

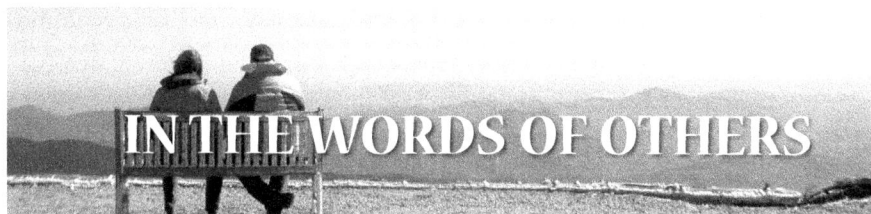

With "1-800-OH-My GOODNESS", Chris Bent offers his thoughts on a variety of topics, in order to amuse, inspire, and challenge any reader. With his witty insight, and perspective forged from life experience, Chris seeks to help us all become better individuals

Michael Hopkins, Attorney, Naples, FL

"In this book Chis is honest and open with the reader. He definitely gives you a lot to ponder. You can't wait to see what he is going to share next."

Dorothy K. Ederer O.P.,
Director of Campus Ministry, St. John Student Center

"Oh my goodness", Chris has again presented a faith filled and thought provoking book. His stream of thought, that often reads more like poetry than prose, will cause you to rethink moments of life in a context of love and promise.

Rev Jean Moorman Brindel, CFRE, AFP, Associate Director of Development,
Emeritus United Theological Seminary, Dayton Ohio

"Honest, incisive, poetic and profound: the writings of Chris Bent. Passion for people, the nation and the world spring from his pages; provocative questions leap from the shortest chapters ever. Silent voices speak in these pages and nothing is to be taken for granted, for life and love run deep between the lines of 1-800-OH-MY-GOODNESS."

Wendy J. Deichmann, PhD, President, United Theological Seminary

This is a book by a man of many directions and passions. Straightforward yet thought provoking. Loyal to his convictions and country. And brave. Sharing. Warrior. Humanitarian.

Jeff Lytle, Editorial Page Editor, Naples Daily News

Chris writes like he lives. As a man of distinction, he is a voice for the poor, a champion of the truth and a friend of strong character and conviction. His word and his service are a blessing to all who encounter him.

Vann R. Ellison, President/CEO, St. Matthew's House, Inc.

Chris Bent is a very unusual person – Navy SEAL, Yale graduate, successful business owner, and radical Christian who is comfortable talking with anyone at any level in society. He doesn't just talk about faith or caring about the poor, Chris actually lives his faith and he works with the poor. His smile is genuine and reflects his deep joy in life, America, hard work, people and (most definitely) God. I have enjoyed reading his writings; they are different, often hard hitting and sometimes maybe even a little wild. Each one gives a fresh perspective on contemporary lives, reflecting Chris' intel - ligence and faith. Chris enjoys moving mountains.

Rev. Dr. Ted Sauter, Senior Pastor, North Naples United Methodist Church

A light, refreshing take on some not so light topics. Wrapped in silliness and wit are serious, social and moral truths that challenge us to be more than ordinary.

Peggy Ryba, Membership Director, North Naples Church, Naples, Florida

As a friend, Chris has helped me understand the inherent conflicts embedded in the language of 'political correctness' and how it attempts, and frequently succeeds, in disguising and defeating the 'truth.' Chris is engaged in a rhetorical battle — we need his insight.

William Lord, a 32-year-veteran Executive Producer and Vice-President of ABC News, and Professor of Journalism at Boston University

Chris is like a modern day prophet, throwing modern day concepts and concerns out there for us to contemplate. The seeds he tosses can land on sand or soil depending on the reader. I suggest you pull up a nice spot in your garden and sit down and read…then allow some of his thoughts to germinate in your life!

Mia Guinan, Owner, Gourmet Gang, Camp Trident, Virginia Beach VA

Chris Bent's extraordinary life has given him a perspective that so very few have. His insight comes not only from his incredible experiences but from his deeply rooted sense of responsibility, caring, and love for others. His thoughtful mind is not on idle, but instead always on overdrive, crystallizing in well thought out words those concepts that would have many times escaped us, were it not for the efforts of this author to engage, care deeply, and then, as Chris has done so remarkably here, write.

Jennifer L. Whitelaw, Attorney, Whitelaw Legal Group, Naples, FL

My nickname for Chris is "Dream-Catcher"- because that's who he is to me. He is my mentor in how to give on His behalf. Freely and generously, Chris offers both words, "God bless you!", and gifts. And all the while he is making a compelling and powerful statement. Chris Bent has discovered a beautiful way to live!

Rev. Dr. Ruth Merriam, The Church on the Cape (U.M.C.),
Cape Porpoise, Maine — Chris's 'other' pastor!

ACKNOWLEDGEMENTS

Writing 1-800-OH-MY-GOODNESS has been more of an emotional journey. Anything emotional is more personal and I guess more private.

The chapters average only 300 words. There is no planned order. You can open the book anywhere and read the 2 pages and get a smile and a frown if you catch the serious challenge.

Maybe these books will be found some day and help others make fewer mistakes.

I have to always acknowledge those who make a difference to me. This is the short list.

There are my daughters, Candice and Courtney, who thought they knew their dad, but really didn't. There is my brilliant wife Christina, who thought she knew her husband..... And then there are my friends from the past whose life journeys I do not fully know, and who do not know me now. For in life it is who we become, not who we were.

So many people inhabit the fabric of our lives. So many played unseen roles in the writing of my four books. 1-800-I-AM-UNHAPPY Vol. 1 & Vol. 2 are good, 1-800-FOR WOMEN-ONLY is fabulous, 1-800-LAUGHING-OUT-LOUD is great and fun…. The next is written and coming out soon, 1-800-FOR-SEALS-ONLY… you have to be certified to read it… LOL

Lastly, there are Sandra Simmons-Dawson and Brian Dawson who helped edit and format the books, website, and marketing. Their firm, Money Management Solutions, Inc. dba Customer Finder Marketing http://customerfindermarketing.com/ is a gem.

www.ingramcontent.com/pod-product-compliance
Lightning Source LLC
Chambersburg PA
CBHW071529040426
42452CB00008B/944